Yale Global Alumni Leadership Exchange presents

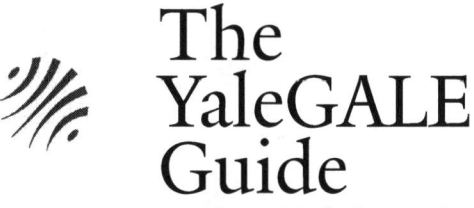

The YaleGALE Guide
to Alumni Relations and Volunteer Engagement

Editor

Ben Slotznick '70, '73 Dra
Chair, Communication Committee YaleGALE

Co-editor

Kathy Edersheim '87
Chair, YaleGALE
Senior Director, Association of Yale Alumni

THE YALEGALE GUIDE

All rights reserved.
Copyright © 2015

graphic design by John Boak '70

TO ALUMNI RELATIONS & VOLUNTEER ENGAGEMENT

The YaleGALE Guide
to Alumni Relations and Volunteer Engagement

A publication of the Yale Global Alumni Leadership Exchange

Letter from Yale President Peter Salovey 10
Preface 13
Acknowledgements 15
Introduction... 19

Part I
An Overview of Alumni Relations at Yale University ... 23

CHAPTER 1 | YALE'S ALUMNI HISTORY 25

1.1   History of Alumni Relations at Yale 25
1.2   Alumni Relations at Yale Today.......................... 27
1.3   Time, Talent, and Treasure 29

CHAPTER 2 | THE ASSOCIATION OF YALE ALUMNI AND
            ITS GOVERNANCE................................ 31

CHAPTER 3 | VOLUNTEER-DRIVEN ALUMNI RELATIONS PROGRAMMING 33

3.1   Class Connections 33
3.2   Yale Clubs 35
    3.2.1   Yale Alumni Community Service Fellowships 36
    3.2.2   Bulldogs Across America 37
    3.2.3   Feb Club Emeritus 38
3.3   Graduate & Professional School Alumni................... 40
    3.3.1   Yale School of Forestry & Environmental Studies 41
3.4   SIGs (shared interest groups or affinity groups) 43
    3.4.1   Sports Associations 44
    3.4.2   Yale Alumni Entrepreneurs 46
    3.4.3   The Yale Alumni Chorus 47
    3.4.4   YaleWomen 48
3.5   Service Programs and Initiatives......................... 49
    3.5.1   Yale Day of Service 49
    3.5.2   Yale Alumni Service Corps 50
    3.5.3   Yale Global Alumni Leadership Exchange 51
3.6   Student-Alumni Initiatives 52

CHAPTER 4 | UNDERGRADUATE ADMISSIONS AND ALUMNI VOLUNTEERS 55

4.1   Admission to Yale and alumni interviewing................ 55
4.2   The Admissions Office and the Alumni Schools Network..... 57
4.3   Yale Alumni Schools Ambassadors 58

CHAPTER 5 | GIVING AT YALE
(THE YALE OFFICE OF DEVELOPMENT AND
THE YALE ALUMNI FUND) 59

5.1 Annual Giving through the Yale Alumni Fund 59
5.2 Capital Campaign Fundraising at Yale 60

Part II
The Process of Organizing Volunteer Communities. . . . 63

CHAPTER 6 | DEVELOPING VOLUNTEERS AND
VOLUNTEER LEADERS 65

6.1 Volunteer Engagement 65
6.2 The 40th Reunion of the Class of 1970 67

CHAPTER 7 | LEADERSHIP CULTIVATION 75

7.1 Nurturing Leaders 75
7.2 Publicly Recognizing Volunteers through awards 78
7.3 Leadership and Governance 80

CHAPTER 8 | ORGANIZING PEOPLE 83

8.1 Affinity Groups 83
8.2 Organizing Alumni by Interests and Passions 85
8.3 Creating a Community around Travel 88
8.4 Building Alumni Community through Athletics 90

CHAPTER 9 | CREATING ORGANIZATIONS 93

9.1 Strategic Planning for an alumni relations organization 93
9.2 Advanced Strategic Planning through bold ideas 96

CHAPTER 10 | DEVELOPING A CULTURE AND SHARED VALUES 101

10.1 Building a Culture of connection and loyalty 101
10.2 Parents as donors and community members 104
10.3 The Architecture of Return 106
    10.3.1 The Campus as a Curated Gallery of fine architecture . . 107
10.4 Building Community through symbol, ritual and tradition. . . 110

CHAPTER 11 | COMMUNICATING 113

11.1 University Communications with Alumni 113
11.2 Effective Use of Social Media 114
11.3 When Volunteers manage and maintain media 117
11.4 Planning Multiple-Location Events using social media 119

Part III
Organizations and Their Planned Events 123

CHAPTER 12 | CLASSES
                 (REUNIONS AND HOMECOMINGS). 125

12.1 Reunions – part 1 126
12.2 Reunions – part 2 129
12.3 Volunteer-run Reunions from the professional's view 131
12.4 Building Attendance at a Reunion 133

CHAPTER 13 | CLUBS AND CHAPTERS
(REGIONAL PROGRAMS) 137

13.1 Programs to Sustain Alumni Engagement 138

 13.1.1 Engaging Alumni of Different Ages 140

 13.1.2 List of sample regional association activities 143

13.2 Student Internships, Mentoring, and alumni participation . . . 145

 13.2.1 Creating a "Bulldogs" Intern Program 147

13.3 Regional Associations Abroad 149

CHAPTER 14 | GRADUATE AND PROFESSIONAL SCHOOLS
(CONVOCATIONS AND COLLOQUIA) 153

14.1 Graduate School Alumni Organizations 153

14.2 Convocations, Conferences, and Colloquia 155

CHAPTER 15 | SHARED INTEREST GROUPS & AFFINITY GROUPS . 159

CHAPTER 16 | SERVICE PROGRAMS & INITIATIVES 161

16.1 Day of Service Abroad 162

16.2 Planning a local Day of Service 164

Part IV
Fundraising 169

CHAPTER 17 | DEVELOPMENT 101 171

17.1 The Fundraising Cycle and Donor Motivation 171

17.2 The Intimate Face of Fundraising 174

17.3 Capital Campaigns 177
17.4 Fundraising with "Friends of" Organizations 179

CHAPTER 18 | THE ROLE OF VOLUNTEERS IN FUNDRAISING. . . . 183

CHAPTER 19 | THE ARC OF GIVING OVER A LIFETIME.......... 187
19.1 Preparing Students for a Lifetime of Giving............... 187
19.2 Keeping the Connection with young alumni 190
19.3 Keeping Alumni Engaged over a lifetime 193

Conclusion..................................... 197

Appendices..................................... 199

Appendix 1 | Bulldogs Across America Data 199
Appendix 2 | Study Guide of discussion topics.................. 201
Appendix 3 | Editor Biographies............................. 210

Praise for The YaleGALE Guide................... 212

TO ALUMNI RELATIONS & VOLUNTEER ENGAGEMENT

THE YALEGALE GUIDE

Yale OFFICE OF THE PRESIDENT

PO BOX 208229
New Haven CT 06520-8229
T 203-432-2550

November 2015

Dear Yale Alumni and Colleagues,

Welcome to the first YaleGALE Guide! Born of the direct experience of the Yale Global Alumni Leadership Exchange, an organization dedicated to the worldwide advancement of education through alumni engagement, this book is designed for alumni leaders, alumni relations professionals, and any institution wishing to inform the efforts of its volunteers.

Since becoming president, I have sought to build a "more unified Yale," one defined by and strengthened through its abiding sense of community. Alumni relations are integral to achieving this, connecting our graduates more closely to the university, to each other, and to the generations of students who follow in their footsteps. None of this would be possible without the dedication of our volunteers, who reinforce the university's shared ideals and foster the deep loyalty that is the hallmark of Yalies around the world.

I take great pride in noting that the alumni who set out to create this guide did so, from the outset, with the goal of supporting volunteer engagement and alumni relations not just at Yale, but at all institutions. The information and advice in the pages that follow were contributed by the alumni themselves — who better to offer insights on what motivates volunteers and how to work with them?

The YaleGALE Guide represents the passion, inspiration, and collective hard work of Yale's alumni volunteers and the staff who support and collaborate with them. As Nathan Hale, a 1773 graduate of Yale College, said: "I wish to be useful." We hope this book will be just that — and that you will share your perspective and ideas with us for future editions.

Sincerely,

Peter Salovey
President
Chris Argyris Professor of Psychology

November 2015

Dear Yale Alumni and Colleagues,

Welcome to the first YaleGALE Guide! Born of the direct experience of the Yale Global Alumni Leadership Exchange, an organization dedicated to the worldwide advancement of education through alumni engagement, this book is designed for alumni leaders, alumni relations professionals, and any institution wishing to inform the efforts of its volunteers.

Since becoming president, I have sought to build a "more unified Yale," one defined by and strengthened through its abiding sense of community. Alumni relations are integral to achieving this, connecting our graduates more closely to the university, to each other, and to the generations of students who follow in their footsteps. None of this would be possible without the dedication of our volunteers, who reinforce the university's shared ideals and foster the deep loyalty that is the hallmark of Yalies around the world.

I take great pride in noting that the alumni who set out to create this guide did so, from the outset, with the goal of supporting volunteer engagement and alumni relations not just at Yale, but at all institutions. The information and advice in the pages that follow were contributed by the alumni themselves – who better to offer insights on what motivates volunteers and how to work with them?

The YaleGALE Guide represents the passion, inspiration, and collective hard work of Yale's alumni volunteers and the staff who support and collaborate with them. As Nathan Hale, a 1773 graduate of Yale College, said: "I wish to be useful." We hope this book will be just that – and that you will share your perspective and ideas with us for future editions.

Sincerely,
Peter Salovey, President
Chris Argyris Professor of Psychology

The YaleGALE Guide

Preface

This book is a response to the enthusiasm with which representatives of hundreds of educational institutions from around the world have greeted exchanges with the Yale Global Alumni Leadership Exchange (YaleGALE), a volunteer driven initiative of the Association of Yale Alumni. Over the past 8 years, the growing demand for meetings, conferences, discussions and exchanges about advancement and alumni support has made it clear that alumni relations – the engagement between graduates and their academic institution – is a life-long relationship of paramount importance.

Strong, internationally competitive universities are essential for innovation and growth. To stay competitive, world leading universities increasingly need to engage with their alumni and develop resources from alumni. Alumni provide crucial leadership by serving as trustees and board members, by giving advice and counsel in their areas of professional expertise, and by acting as volunteer "consultants" to the management team at a university. Universities, both private and public, have a growing dependence on financial contributions from alumni for financial support. Alumni associations are key to successful fundraising efforts – so vital to the long term growth of our institutions.

Just as importantly, as a university's alumni become scattered across the globe, alumni themselves become more important than ever for creating, organizing and implementing programs that bring alumni together and inspire their loyalty to university. Alumni as volunteers for – and on behalf of – the university are an often underutilized resource. And alumni as leaders of alumni volunteer efforts – whether developing programs or asking for money – are even more so.

There are surprisingly few resources about the concept of alumni relations or how to create a robust alumni relations program. There are even fewer resources for anyone wanting to learn about working with and inspiring alumni volunteers. CASE (the Council for Advancement and Support of Education, an industry organization) does provide informative resources about alumni relations to its members. The material in this Guide is different because it is written by inspired alumni volunteers based on their experiences as volunteers and leaders on behalf of their university.

As explained more fully in the Guide, YaleGALE, founded in 2007, itself reflects the trend to have deeper and more fulfilling opportunities for alumni to connect with their own institution and to serve others. The individual pieces for this Guide were written by volunteers in that YaleGALE spirit. A spirit which is both educational and collaborative.

YaleGALE has been producing written resource materials since 2008. The first effort to prepare supporting documentation for an exchange was the YaleGALE Resource Book. Volunteer leaders participating in the trip each wrote a piece for the Resource Book to share their motivation and inspiration for being a volunteer leader and to provide useful examples of alumni relations information. Over several years the Resource Book grew in length and in purpose, and now stands at over 100 pages. (See *www.yalegale.org/resources/wp-content/uploads/2012/08/ResourceBook2012.pdf* .) That Book inspired this Guide.

The more YaleGALE traveled, the more supporting material proved useful. YaleGALE Exchanges added new topics of discussion and attracted more people looking for specific guidance and new ideas. Beginning with YaleGALE's visit to China in 2011, participants created written descriptions of specific alumni programs. With each Conference or Exchange, there were new topics for the presentations and the discussions which demanded supporting material. Now, there is more than enough material to produce a book. We hope it will be helpful to alumni interested in volunteering and to the alumni relations professionals interested in working with them. The YaleGALE Guide will never replace the exchanges and the interpersonal interactions that are so necessary for building a community, however we hope it serves as a lasting resource for exchanges and a regular resource for ideas for professionals and volunteers.

Acknowledgements

This Guide is an act of serendipity, but also inevitable. It has been created from the articulated writings, informed discussions, and demonstrated leadership of the hundreds of dedicated Yale alumni volunteers involved in the Yale Global Alumni Leadership Exchange (YaleGALE) since 2007.

Many of the written descriptions of specific alumni programs were written by YaleGALE participants in anticipation of the YaleGALE visit to China in 2011. With some revisions and additions, these have become an important part of YaleGALE's online resources. (See *www.yalegale. org/resources/overview-of-yale-volunteering* .) Almost one hundred Yale alumni, family, and friends participated in the YaleGALE trip to China. Part I of this Guide is largely their work for which the editors of this Guide are greatly appreciative.

Subsequently, YaleGALE created additional supplemental written material. Several handouts to support session topics were created for the 2013 YaleGALE conference in Paris, hosted by the U.S. Embassy. Another group were created for the Yale Global Alumni Leadership Forum (@Yale) in the fall of 2013. Several more for the YaleGALE trip to Europe in spring of 2014. Many more for YaleGALE @Yale in the fall of 2014 and 2015. Plus several more for the YaleGALE conferences in India in January 2015. (See *www.yalegale.org/resources/handouts* .) These materials compose the vast majority of Parts II, III, and IV of this Guide. Well over a hundred Yale alumni, family, and friends have participated in YaleGALE trips and programs since China. The latter part of this Guide owes a debt to them all.

In addition to the editors' deep gratitude to the hundreds of Yale alumni volunteers whose passionate involvement in YaleGALE exchanges, forums, and conferences has made this Guide possible, there are some individuals for whom special thanks is warranted.

First, we have to acknowledge Mark Dollhopf '77, Executive Director of the Association of Yale Alumni during the first seven years of YaleGALE, and before that an extraordinary volunteer founder of the Yale Alumni Chorus. At Yale, he championed notions of shared interest groups and pioneered service initiatives – providing innovative ways for alumni to engage with the university. These two notions of service and shared interests (though distinct, separate, and with their own organizational histories) are both at the very heart of the passion which unites YaleGALE volunteers – and without which YaleGALE would not exist. This Guide owes much to Mark's articulation of many concepts: a culture of giving, the three "T"s (time, talent, and treasure), friend-raising versus fundraising … the list goes on. And it owes much to the inspiring way he presents these ideas. Mark is an exceptional motivational speaker – and makes one aspire to do in text what he does in person. Thanks, Mark.

In addition, we want to especially thank the other volunteer producers of YaleGALE trips abroad: Marv Berenblum '56 and Sharon Houle Randall '98. Both have contributed writing and inspiration to this labor. They have always been available when needed.

Of the many other volunteers who have contributed time and talent to the YaleGALE venture, we want to recognize Roy Niedermayer '69, Stuart Cohen '70, and Ed Sevilla '82, who have always written when requested, and helped when asked. Other contributors include Paul Broholm '78, Thatcher Shellaby '70, John Boak '70, Donna Consolini, Jennifer Julier '77, Nike Irvin '85, Kate Philip '10, Katy Wells '91 J.D., Jack Thomas '80, Bobbi Mark '76, Randy Helm '70, Ian Glenday '70, Ken Inadomi '76, Xiaoyan Huang '91, Greg Prince, Jr. '61, '73 Ph.D., and Susie Krentz '80.

A special shout out to Lynn Andrewsen '82, Managing Director of the Yale Alumni Fund. She has been involved in this Guide since before it was one – and with YaleGALE since China. She has written, edited, supervised, or polished just about everything YaleGALE has produced on fundraising.

We would like especially to thank Yale President Peter Salovey '86 Ph.D., for his leadership and vision, inspiring alumni to be engaged and to support the university.

Thanks also to John Boak '70 for graphic design and cover art, and Stephen Morris '70 of ThePublicPress.com for shepherding this book to publication.

With this wealth of actionable, first-hand information, written with such enthusiasm, a book was inevitable. That it is taking this form and at this time is the serendipity.

Of course, all errors and omissions are the responsibility of the editors.

Editor:

Ben Slotznick '70, '73 Dra

Chair, Communication Committee, YaleGALE

Co-editor:

Kathy Edersheim '87

Chair, YaleGALE

Senior Director, Association of Yale Alumni

Note from the Editors: You may have noticed the inclusion of identifying numbers after the name of each Yale alumnus or alumna. Further emphasizing the sometimes compulsive identification with Yale by its alumni, we choose to self-identify by our year of graduation and our degree earned. That number indicates the year of graduation, most often from Yale College. For someone who attended Yale for graduate or professional school, the school or degree will be indicated after the year.

THE YALEGALE GUIDE

Introduction

The heart of this book is about volunteers – recruiting them, inspiring them, helping them organize, nurturing their development into leaders, and helping them to succeed. Volunteering for Yale and on behalf of Yale has enriched the lives of all the contributors to this book – so volunteering in alumni relations is both the inspiration and the framework within which this book has been created. Just as we have been inspired to volunteer, we hope that you will be inspired with new ideas based on this Guide.

The material in this book has been written by many alumni volunteers. It expresses the hard-won knowledge gained from their years of volunteering experience. The individual sections were written over a number of years by different authors for particular YaleGALE exchanges, conferences and discussion panels. This inevitably means that different sections are written in somewhat different styles, and some of the material is covered from multiple directions and somewhat different viewpoints – but the editors believe that this adds to the richness of this material and the lessons it imparts.

This also means that the opinions expressed in this book are an amalgam of those of YaleGALE alumni volunteers. They are not the opinions of Yale University or the Association of Yale Alumni.

Part I provides the context for volunteering primarily by discussing programs and structures from alumni relations at Yale and specifically the Association of Yale Alumni (AYA). These articles reflect the experiences of the contributors – Yale's alumni leaders, all participants in the Yale Global Alumni Leadership Exchange (YaleGALE). Additionally, many of the contributors are volunteer leaders for other organizations in their communities, and have provided insights from those experiences as well. While reading this wealth of information on alumni relations, we encourage you to think about the concepts as well as the specifics as they can be applied to other volunteer organizations.

Yale has a long history in the field of alumni relations, and many standard practices in the field were pioneered at Yale by alumni volunteers. At Yale, the culture of active alumni giving back to university grew organically, and often outside the University's purview. Yale also has a long history of student volunteering, so has much to share about developing a community that values giving back. There are lessons to be learned from this. For this reason, Part I provides a blend of context for alumni relations as well as summaries of a number of Yale's successful programs and initiatives.

Most of all, there is one overarching principle that we have learned from participating in YaleGALE – one crucial thing that sharing our experiences with others from around the world has taught us. There is no one right way to do alumni relations. There are many best ways. They depend on the history and culture in which an institution is embedded.

Part II focuses on volunteers and volunteering directly. It discusses how to find volunteers, nurture them, and develop organizations around them. It is intended to help professionals work with and advise volunteers. Perhaps more importantly, it is designed to help volunteer leaders grow in their leadership roles, and build community among the other volunteers with whom they work.

As an executive summary of Part II, here are the main points.

❑ Ask people what they want to do, and help them make it happen.

❑ Bring people together to help them fulfill their passions.

❑ Thank them – and thank them again.

Over and over, in different circumstances, these precepts will prove fundamental. Certainly, an organization's leaders must ensure that volunteer efforts contribute towards and are driven by the organization's mission. In terms of implementing the mission, these three principles are the key to working with volunteers.

Part III is a follow up to the more general discussion of volunteering in Part II. It delves into more specific considerations of how volunteers can energize particular programs and projects. It looks in more detail at the particular organizational components of alumni activities (at AYA and elsewhere). And it examines how volunteers responsible for these components can plan and implement various types of events and programming. It's where the rubber hits the road.

Part IV of the Guide discusses how volunteers can be an integral part of fundraising efforts – as they are at the Yale Alumni Fund and elsewhere. The history of fundraising at Yale began with alumni volunteers – when the university was appreciative of the efforts, but not so directly involved in the enterprise. Much has evolved in the past hundred years, and the field is now largely run by highly trained professionals. However, the non-professional and volunteer are still essential. They may identify prospects for the professional to develop and they coordinate a base level of giving among a broad community which the professionals can leverage among the top givers. We at YaleGALE are acutely aware that many of those interested in expanding their alumni relations programming hope such efforts will improve their fundraising endeavors.

However, for an institution's development efforts to reach their full potential, the institution must forge and then nurture a sense of community among the potential donors – from the time they are students. It must assist alumni in their efforts to "give back", whether time, money or expertise, from the time before they were alumni – when they were just students – and over a lifetime. The institution must recognize that it takes a lifetime of cultivation for students and alumni to develop into significant donors. Integrating volunteers into the development efforts can make that happen.

Thank you for your interest in our book. We hope it helps develop a successful volunteer effort.

THE YaleGALE Guide

Part I

An Overview of Alumni Relations at Yale University

The relationship of a university with its alumni is unique to the institution and constantly evolving. Alumni relations at Yale grew organically from alumni volunteer efforts that created programs with the institution providing support in response to alumni interests and their interest in supporting the institution. This is part of its history and effects its shape and contour today. We realize that starting, bolstering, or re-building an alumni organization nowadays will take a different path – and produce a different organization – one most suited to the institution.

Nonetheless, there is value in describing many of the features of alumni relations at Yale as well as its specific alumni relations programs. The chapters in this part of the Guide provide descriptions, all in one place and from a single viewpoint, that of their volunteers. This allows you, the reader, to more easily compare and contrast them. It allows you to see the common elements that appeal over and over, in various permutations, to alumni participants and alumni volunteers. It allows you to examine the unique elements of each program – as perceived by alumni volunteers – that draw alumni to particular programs. We realize that any one of these programs – as currently in place – might not be useful or appropriate for your university. But parts of them might. These overviews let you evaluate which parts of these programs might be adaptable to your culture and its institutions.

Chapter 1

Yale's Alumni History

The history of alumni relations at Yale provides the context for where we are today and may provide some inspiration for other institutions. Yale University was founded in 1701 with one student and even that plays a significant role in the current structure of Yale alumni relations. Yale is now composed of an undergraduate college with approximately 5,400 students, plus graduate and professional schools with another 6,500. It has approximately 150,000 living alumni.

Today, many departments at Yale interact with alumni with certain areas having specific responsibilities and goals:

❏ the Association of Yale Alumni (the organization that focuses on alumni relations)

❏ the Office of Development (the fundraising arm of the University)

❏ the Athletic Department (which shepherds alumni programs involved with former athletes), and

❏ the Office of Admissions for undergraduates (which relies upon alumni volunteers to help recruit students).

1.1 | History of Alumni Relations at Yale

This chronology traces the development of alumni organization at Yale over more than two centuries. Several aspects of alumni activity appear to have originated at Yale and were emulated later at other institutions. And, when Yale was not the first institution to establish certain alumni relationships programs, it was never far behind.

The first college to identify classes. Yale is thought to be the first college to have identified its alumni on the basis of their affiliation with specific undergraduate classes back in 1792, still the most common concept in organizing alumni affairs in the U.S today. In 1824 one-half of the graduating class of 1821 returned to New Haven at Commencement by common agreement to receive an M.A. degree, a practice derived from the English system. Although graduates from Yale's earliest days also had returned to receive their M.A. degrees three or more years after receiving their first degree, the tradition established by the Class of 1821 strengthened a cycle of triennial reunions that eventually was refined into the five-year or "quinquennial" system of class reunions known today.

Yale's first alumni organization. "The Society of the Alumni" was formed with the avowed object of "sustaining and advancing the interests of the college" in 1827. The Society of Alumni was a membership organization "confined to graduates who paid at least two dollars annually to the funds of the college." An outgrowth of earlier alumni affairs activities, this was the first of many refinements in the formal organization of alumni affairs to follow. After two years no record of its existence could be found, but in August of 1842 The Society of the Alumni of Yale College re-emerged at a general meeting of the graduates. In its reincarnation, the organization broadened its platform by accepting "all graduates of the institution, in virtue of their graduation" as members of the Society, a policy which now encompasses anyone who has completed one semester of a degree granting program at Yale.

Yale's first shared interest group. The earliest origins of what Yale calls Shared Interest Groups (also affinity groups) came in 1853 when students and alumni gathered in the interest of rowing and formed the "Yale Navy."

The longest continuing regional club. In 1864, the Cincinnati Alumni Association was established, becoming the first regional Yale club and, it is believed, the longest continuing regional club of any college or university. In the next few years, other Yale clubs were founded in the U.S. and internationally.

It took more than 100 years and many experimental structures until Yale decided to fund a central structure with a volunteer representative governing body for alumni activities in 1971. At the time, the Association of Yale Alumni had four stated purposes, namely: to maintain the status of the University; to provide a channel of mutual communication between the alumni and the University; to oversee the direction of all alumni organizations and programs; and to provide the means (when appropriate) for the explication and forthright examination of University policies, in order that the University position be explained to the Assembly and appropriate recommendations advanced to the Corporation.

Ambassadors for Yale. In the past 45 years, the AYA has expanded its mission as reflected in the Strategic Plan adopted in 2007 "Ambassadors for Yale" emphasizing the importance of calling alumni to service on behalf of Yale as well as for Yale. The plan also recognizes the importance of Shared Interest Groups as well as Classes and Regional Associations. The AYA further emphasized the role of volunteers on behalf of Yale with the "Ambassadors in Action" Strategic Plan of 2012.

1.2 | Alumni Relations at Yale Today

Membership in AYA. At Yale, alumni relations are conducted through the Association of Yale Alumni known as AYA. AYA includes everyone who attended Yale for at least one semester of a degree-granting program. No dues or fees are charged for membership. The AYA is managed by a professional staff, but it is governed by representatives of the alumni. Many of its initiatives are driven by alumni interests and alumni determination.

The AYA connects alumni to each other and to the university through four primary avenues, three that are obvious outcomes of the history.

- ❑ Regional clubs or associations
- ❑ Shared interest groups, also called affinity groups or SIGs.
- ❑ Graduate and Professional School alumni associations
- ❑ Yale College Classes (based upon year of graduation)

Regional Clubs or Associations. Regional clubs were the second initiative of alumni when they began to self-organize in the 19th century. There are now Yale Clubs in 40 countries plus 149 geographic regions of the USA. Yale Clubs connect alumni for continuing education, social events, and networking. Yale Clubs promote Yale by organizing volunteering opportunities in their communities, where alumni perform charitable acts together. And Yale Clubs include alumni from all branches of the University whether the College, the Professional Schools or the Graduate School of Arts and Sciences.

Shared Identity/Interest Groups (SIGs), originally groups of alumni self-organized to provide financial support (and sometimes adult guidance) for specific shared extra-curricular interests, have become the fastest growing area of engagement for Yale Alumni. Yale graduates have been coming together on the basis of a "shared identity", related to ethnicity, religion, or culture. Such groups include the Association of Asian-American Yale Alumni and YaleWomen. Alumni have also begun to organize groups around a "shared interest" that developed after graduation, such as a common professional interest. The Yale in Real Estate Association is an example. The shared interest may even be something done while a student which continues during adulthood. For example, the Yale Alumni Chorus travels around the world giving concerts.

Graduate and professional schools. Yale has 13 graduate and professional schools so each school has its own alumni that are also part of the University alumni body. Graduate and Professional Alumni are invited to and are active in AYA activities, including regional clubs, national programs, and international ones such as YaleGALE.

In addition, the Graduate and Professional Schools have their own alumni events. Examples include convocations, colloquia, and reunions. They have communication channels and strategies similar to the classes. They work on developing similar connections.

Yale Class alumni activities were the earliest alumni activities started over two centuries ago. They were based upon those who went to Yale for an undergraduate education – and who graduated in the same year – members of the same graduating class.

Yes, classmates scatter after graduation, but class officers work to preserve and strengthen the friendships of youth. They relay news of marriages, career successes, children and deaths. They do this through class notes published in the Alumni Magazine. They may use class websites, email list-serves, blogs and Facebook pages to stay connected. In addition, every five years, the class works with the professional team at AYA to hold a multi-day reunion back at the University.

As part of the Strategic Plans, AYA and alumni volunteers have developed new service projects and initiatives. Alumni are finding more and more ways to connect and AYA has been helping them do so. But many of the newest efforts involve a shared interest in serving others – building a common connection among alumni while doing "good deeds" together.

We hope this has provided a bird's-eye view of alumni relations at Yale, and how the programs connect. The rest of Part I will look more closely at many of them. In addition to greater detail, we will be discussing who volunteers for a program, why they volunteer, and what Yale gets out of it. You can find edited versions of these overviews (with pictures) on the YaleGALE Resources website.

1.3 | Time, Talent, and Treasure

A culture of giving. This book will often invoke the notion of a "culture of giving" or "giving back" or "paying it forward". Importantly, this is not just about money. It recognizes that people can serve by giving their time and talent as well. Sometimes, the gift of time or talent is more crucial than funds. It is a gift everyone can contribute, and often binds a community more strongly than the gift of treasure as alumni have so much more that they can give. Often the gift of time and talent will lead to a gift of treasure.

Mark Dollhopf '77, formerly Executive Director of the AYA, often calls alumni relations the job of friend-raising. At Yale, this friend-raising is separated from fundraising. As mentioned, the fundraising is conducted and managed by a separate organization, the Yale Office of Development.

Fundraising and friend-raising are separate tasks, but with many connections. For example, both tasks use many alumni volunteers

– and many of these volunteers participate in both activities – though often at different times. Interestingly, both the AYA and the Yale Alumni Fund (the most broad-based volunteer aspect of the Development Office) have approximately 100 volunteers for every member of the staff. This demonstrates how integral alumni volunteers are to all efforts that support Yale, and how volunteers giving time, talent and treasure provide a multiplier effect to university efforts in both Friend-raising and Fundraising.

Early fundraising at Yale. As Yale was supported in the early 1700s by gifts from Elihu Yale, so began the culture of giving treasure. In 1831, Yale announced its first organized effort to raise significant funds for endowment, the Centum Millia Fund drive, with the objective of raising $100,000 in one year from Yale alumni, faculty, parents and friends of the University.

The Yale Alumni Fund. Considerably later in 1890, in response to "a widespread sentiment among Yale graduates in favor of some systematic endeavor to increase the resources of the University," the Corporation voted to establish an "Alumni University Fund." Known now as the Yale Alumni Fund, this was the first organized effort to secure annual contributions to augment the operating budget. It is only for the past 30 years that Yale has had a full time development staff.

Chapter 2

The Association of Yale Alumni and its governance

The structure of alumni volunteer governance. The Association of Yale Alumni consists of everyone who has completed at least one semester of a degree granting program at Yale University. No dues or fees are expected. The affairs of the AYA are managed by a professional staff who are employees of Yale University and advised or "governed" by the AYA Board of Governors and more loosely by the Assembly of delegates.

The Assembly is a representative body of Yale alumni selected by supporting Yale alumni organizations around the world. The Assembly meets one time per year on the Yale campus to discuss alumni affairs, volunteering for Yale, and the affairs of the university. Members of the Assembly are called "delegates" and often have served Yale as volunteer alumni leaders in their local communities, their Yale interest or identity groups.

The Assembly elects a Board of Governors from its membership. The AYA Board of Governors consists of 30 alumni volunteers with demonstrated interest in leadership. The Board meets several times per year and works closely with the AYA professional staff. Members of the AYA Board serve for three years. The Board elects five officers, including a Chair of the Board.

Volunteers in governance. Members of the AYA Assembly and the AYA Board of Governors are selected by their peers for their leadership skills and for their passion to serve Yale. Alumni of every age may serve. Alumni of every professional background may serve.

The role of alumni leaders. Leaders in AYA governance, members of the AYA Board of Governors, develop the vision and the strategies that inspire Yale alumni to serve Yale, and they communicate that information broadly, including over the internet. Second, they work with the professional team to support the broad array of activities and programs that engage the alumni around the world. This will include attending meetings and organizing and attending events and programs.

The benefits to alumni and to Yale. Volunteer alumni leadership helps Yale achieve its goal of providing service to the global community. Volunteer leadership helps alumni support each other, which builds a community across generations who share a common goal of service and strengthening Yale.

The Association of Yale Alumni. The Association of Yale Alumni is the current governing structure of Yale alumni activity. Yale alumni activity began in 1792 – the longest record of any American university. The organization and content of Yale alumni activities have evolved over the centuries. Many if not most of these changes were conceived and implemented by alumni volunteers although there is now significant professionalization of alumni relations. Volunteers continue to be the key to success.

Chapter 3

Volunteer-driven Alumni Relations Programming

Most alumni related programming at Yale is offered through the Association of Yale Alumni. Alumni volunteers manage much of this under a variety of programs. Professional staff at AYA generally act as consultants and advisors although in some cases they also provide essential coordination. This section provides more details on the volunteer-driven programs and the roles of the volunteers.

In addition, AYA provides some services directly to alumni without volunteer input, such as the travel and education programs through Yale Educational Travel as well as the Yale affinity credit card.

Yale University itself offers programming directly to its graduates. Examples include free online courses and podcasts, low cost university course auditing at Yale, individually scheduled visits by professors and senior administrators to major cities (often coordinated through AYA), and spectator access to university sports events. The University also cooperates with the AYA in many of its program offerings. However, the vast majority of alumni relations at Yale is volunteer driven. Here are some representative examples of the programs.

3.1 | Class Connections
friendships based on year of graduation

The Class connection starts as undergraduates. From the moment a student is accepted to Yale, he or she becomes affiliated with a graduating class year. Before the first year at Yale begins, there is a week-long orientation for class members. Students live with other members of their class and participate in rich class traditions sponsored by the university throughout their time at Yale, ranging from the Freshman Dinner during their first year at Yale to Senior Week at the end of their last. During undergraduate years, each class has a leadership council to arrange activities for members of that class. Class members experience arrival at the university together, the same four years of cultural and social events at the university, and they plan for their post-university lives together. Class members will have shared memories of being a university student based on remembering world events, popular contemporary music, and fashions trends. Class members have memories of four years together that no other person can share in quite the same way.

The organizational structure of the class. Every five years, each class elects two officers. The Class Secretary reports news of classmates and the Class Treasurer collects money for class activities. Sometimes a group of representatives, a Class Council, helps the class officers. The first Secretary and Treasurer are elected just prior to the final year at the university, allowing class leadership to take root before graduation.

Class activities after graduation. Classmates scatter after graduation, so communication through class officers preserves and strengthens friendships. The Secretary relays news of marriages, career successes, children and deaths through class notes published in the Yale Alumni Magazine. Officers and others may use class websites, email list-serves, blogs and Facebook pages to stay connected. Every five years, the class holds a multi-day reunion back at the university: listening to lectures or touring new facilities, meeting friends, dancing to music from university days. Some classes have gatherings between reunion years.

The Class nurtures a strong and flexible personal network. The Class provides lifelong connections to peers. Because it cuts across academic majors and specific interests, it provides links to a broad and diverse range of resources. When these enrich your life or career you will feel loyalty – and obligation – to your class and your university.

3.2 | Yale Clubs
regional groups and associations

Geographical bridges. In 40 countries and 149 geographic regions of the USA, diverse groups of alumni representing a spectrum of age groups, genders, professional schools, ethnic or religious heritages, sexual orientations and shared interest groups gather to share their common experience at Yale. While almost half of all alumni reside in New York, Washington, New Haven, Boston, Chicago, San Francisco, and Los Angeles, regional groups exist throughout the USA and the world, providing links to Yale, serving their communities, promoting Yale through interviewing applicants for Yale, and providing continuing education opportunities for Yale alumni where they live.

Yale regional alumni seek to change lives by serving and improving their own communities. With this focus, alumni work and gather together, sharing and enhancing the leadership strengths gained from Yale education. Regional associations are financially independent from Yale and autonomously manage their regional governance, programs and events.

Emphasizing young people. Regional Yale alumni present Yale Book and Service Awards for secondary school students exhibiting "intellectual promise and outstanding character." Applicants to Yale College receive an individual interview by their local alumni. Alumni groups sponsor summer community service internships for students from Yale. Yale Day of Service projects attract alumni of all ages, their families and their friends.

Continuing education. Regional alumni groups promote lifelong learning experiences as a habit, not merely an ideal, through presentations by noted Yale professors, prominent leaders, and artists, performances by Yale musicians or dramatists, online academic courses, and practical learning through service project experiences designed to stimulate active intellectual engagement, year after year.

Talent and Time, more than Treasure. Financial contributions to Yale are only one reason or purpose for Regional Associations. In addition to using their own funds to support financial aid for students from their local communities, associations work with fellow alumni to improve community conditions, provide continuing education, and foster closer relationships among Yale graduates and commitment to Yale.

An offer to help. Yale's Regional groups (Clubs or Associations) are often pleased to offer friendship and mutual assistance to alumni of foreign universities who wish to explore regional group development in their own country and the USA.

3.2.1 | Yale Alumni Community Service Fellowships

History. The Yale Alumni Community Service Fellowship (YACSF) program was launched in 1989 by a group of Yale alumni who, in response to student interest, began a paid, eight-week public service fellowship meant to offer opportunities to all Yale students to participate in community service over the summer academic break, even if their financial situations might not allow them the chance to engage in unpaid volunteer work. In June 1990, thirteen students fanned out across the United States to fulfill fellowships; one single alumnus agreed to provide the funding for all the fellowships in first summer.

Since that time, nearly 500 students have participated in the YACSF program, with as many as 40 opportunities offered in a single summer. Many past fellows have gone on to found and manage their own nonprofit organizations, as well as become YACSF sponsors in succeeding years.

Structure. Yale Alumni Clubs (or other sponsoring entities) approach nonprofits to determine whether they would like a summer intern, whose salary would be paid by the Club. Interested nonprofits submit applications detailing summer projects to Yale. Students review the applications and apply for positions. Once selected for a fellowship, students undertake meaningful assignments. In the fall, they write reports on their service learning experiences.

Success. In 2008, Alison Gilmeister was a Summer Fellow at KIPP's Will Academy in Washington, DC. She graduated from Yale in 2009 and accepted a full-time job with KIPP as a teaching resident. Allison's summer fellowship laid the groundwork for her future employment at KIPP DC.

Impact. The YACSF is a particularly strong model because it serves to link several key constituencies into one program: Students, alumni, university administrators, and community-based organizations. For all involved, the relationship strengthens not only the general spirit of community service, but more specifically the good will of all toward the institution that facilitates the work, Yale.

3.2.2 | Bulldogs Across America

Changing the lives of Yale students – one internship at a time. Bulldogs Across America is a unique paid 10-week summer internship program for Yale University students. Started in 1999 in Louisville, Kentucky with Bulldogs in the Bluegrass, the program has since expanded to include Cleveland, San Francisco, Denver, Houston, Minneapolis, New Orleans, Santa Fe and St. Louis. Currently, more than 500 Yale students submit over 1,800 applications per year. About 10% of each graduating class participates in at least one Bulldog city. To date, over 1,060 Yale students have participated in a Bulldogs program across the country, and over 85 have moved to a Bulldog city after graduation.

The program attracts talented students to work for business, not-for-profit, and government organizations. The program provides challenging paid internships, introductions to the community and its leaders, alumni mentors, and interesting events. The summer is meaningful for Yale students, alumni, and the local community.

What makes Bulldogs special? Local Yale alumni work hard to provide free housing for interns. Each Bulldog is assigned an adult mentor, often their first true adult friend beyond the family. This leads to life changing relationships as Bulldogs reap the benefit of their mentor's life experiences. The free group housing releases interns from additional financial concerns, and encourages an environment where Bulldogs form lifelong peer friendships. Weekly events feature political and business leaders. Weekends are spent taking advantage of local festivals and attractions.

Why do we do it? Bulldogs pushes students to grow as young adults, building confidence through experience. With over 340 alumni sponsors actively engaged as program leaders, mentors, and contributors, it is a time to reconnect with current life at Yale, provide counsel and work experiences, help showcase their hometown to future residents, and build a vibrant local alumni community. It is the ultimate expression of the value of their Yale education applied locally.

Multiple university summer intern programs. The Bulldogs Across America programs in Cleveland, Ohio and Denver, Colorado have expanded to include other universities. Denver cooperates with Yale, Harvard, Stanford, MIT universities and Middlebury College. The Cleveland program hosts up to 75 students during the summer, and Denver has almost 30 each summer. A multiple university program allows several alumni associations and universities less organized than Yale to participate. For more information visit the website: *www.bulldogsacrossamerica.com* .

3.2.3 | Feb Club Emeritus

What is Feb Club? In 2008, a small group of Yale alumni were bemoaning the fact that their busy lives did not allow them the chance to just hang out with their Yale friends. What they needed was a stress-free, easy and fun way to get together. What they built was Feb Club Emeritus. Feb Club Emeritus is a series of parties for Yalies around the world. Each night of February, there is at least one party. On most nights, there are many. From Atlanta to Zanzibar, and everywhere in between, over 100 events each year draw over 5000 Yalies. This is during what everyone remembers as one of the worst months of the winter in New Haven on the Yale Campus. (To alleviate the February doldrums, there have been student versions of Feb Club since the mid-1970s.)

How a Feb Club party is organized. Local individual hosts are in charge of organizing each event. They can represent local Yale Clubs, local chapters of SIGs, a group of Yale friends, or just a Yale alum who likes to host Yale parties. The parties have three rules: 1) No speeches; 2) No fundraising; and 3) It's just a party. The "Ministry" of Feb Club maintains a website that lists each event and helps hosts keep track of attendance. It coordinates with the Association of Yale Alumni, local Yale Clubs and uses social media to publicize its events.

The parties are as diverse as the locations. The Yale Club of New York throws a kick-off event that routinely draws close to 1,000 attendees. Yalies in Hawaii throw Feb Club on a beach. London Elis go to a pub, while their French classmates sip wine. Some events are large, many are small, all are different. In its first 7 years, Feb Club Emeritus has had over 500 parties, held events on every continent and has drawn over 35,000 guests from the Yale College Classes of 1941 through 2014, as well as graduate and professional schools.

A way to engage – or re-engage. Feb Club Emeritus has become known among Yale alumni groups as an annual social hub. Many Yale clubs use them to attract those who otherwise are not interested in alumni gatherings. Half of the attendees in Atlanta the first year of Feb Club had not been to a Yale event since leaving campus. We hear the same thing time and again. That the promise of no speeches and no fundraising is a draw. As is the fun and, ultimately, the people.

A benefit to Yale. Feb Club Emeritus has turned into a rallying point, drawing people into (or back into) the Yale alumni fold. Some come for the party, and check back in once a year. Others find connections and become involved.

A benefit to Clubs. The distributed nature of Feb Club events, in both location and time, gives needed flexibility to local Clubs – especially small Clubs. Many clubs (and local chapters of SIGs) have large regions that they cover – and parts of those regions have a low density of alumni. This makes it very difficult to schedule, plan, or budget for events to serve all of a region's constituents. In contrast, a Club (or SIG) can work with its scattered members to hold several small Feb Club events across its region – even on different days. For example, the Colorado Yale Assoc. has sponsored as many as seven Feb Club events around the state during February of one year.

3.3 | Graduate & Professional School Alumni

The AYA represents all alumni. The Association of Yale Alumni represents all Yale alumni, including those who earned advanced degrees from the Graduate School of Arts and Sciences or any one of the 13 professional schools at Yale. Each of the graduate and professional schools has at least three delegate slots to the annual AYA Assembly. Their alumni serve on the AYA Board of Governors. There, a dedicated Graduate & Professional Schools Committee focuses on the particular interests of these alumni and their schools. This committee brings matters relating to the graduate and professional schools to the attention of the Board as a whole.

Graduate and Professional School alumni are active in AYA activities. Alumni of the Graduate and Professional Schools are active participants in a broad range of activities within the AYA, such as Yale Day of Service, Yale Alumni Service Corps, the Yale Global Alumni Leadership Exchange, and the Yale Career Network. Some of these are organized on a national level by the AYA. Others are organized on a local or regional basis by local Yale Clubs or SIGs.

Graduate and Professional Schools also have their own alumni events. The Graduate School of Arts and Sciences and most of Yale's professional schools have active alumni programs of their own, each with its own governing board of alumni. Many of these alumni programs have their own schedule of activities such as convocations, colloquia, or "quinquennial" reunions (a reunion of all classes at five-year intervals, e.g. the 2015 reunion will include classes from 2010, 2005, 2000, 1995, etc.).

These events are often organized around symposia and other continuing education opportunities – focused on the specialties of the school. Though these activities are designed for alumni of a particular graduate or professional school, many are open to other alumni from throughout the Yale community.

Alumni enrichment through university-wide programs. The Association of Yale Alumni is a leader among major universities in its commitment to inclusiveness and integration of all of Yale's alumni – undergraduate, graduate, and professional – in a wide array of alumni-led volunteer programs. This leads to increased opportunities for alumni service, networking, and involvement throughout their careers and lives.

3.3.1 | Yale School of Forestry & Environmental Studies

Overview. The Yale School of Forestry & Environmental Studies (F&ES) Alumni Association exists to connect its alumni with all parts of the School and Yale University – building bridges to faculty, students and staff – and to promote and support connections among alumni by class year, area of professional interest and geographic location. The School grants masters and doctorate degrees and has over 4500 alumni. F&ES enrollment consists of over 300 students who have finished their undergraduate education.

Organization. The F&ES Alumni Association membership includes every living graduate of the School. Supported by the F&ES Office of Development and Alumni Services, the work of the Association falls under the leadership of the Alumni Association Board – alumni volunteers who are elected annually by the alumni at large to serve three-year terms. These volunteers meet virtually and in person eight to ten times a year. The Board is governed by elected officers, President, Vice President, Secretary and Treasurer.

A decade ago, a few alumni leaders and a single-person alumni affairs staff undertook and completed a comprehensive strategic plan to serve as a common vision and to inspire broader alumni involvement. The alumni board was enlarged and diversified to create an array of new opportunities for alumni volunteer activities. A quinquennial reunion was instituted for the first time in the school's history and it has quickly grown into far more than a reunion – it provides an array of programs and activities, including seminars featuring leading speakers addressing some of the most pressing environmental challenges of our era, and drawing alumni and students from throughout the university community. The F&ES alumni association reaches out to alumni from across the country and around the world, using new media to make it possible for a much broader and more diverse group of alumni to engage and stay involved.

The alumni board recently modified its constitution and bylaws to institute fixed board terms, term limits, and a standing nominating committee to involve as many alums as possible as board members and keep the board itself continually refreshed with new people, fresh ideas, and representation from younger classes, older classes, and current students. The alumni board proactively engages students as active alums even before they graduate, and gives them reason to stay involved. The board has significantly increased the percentage of alums supporting the School through annual giving.

The F&ES alumni association has transformed itself from being a perfunctory body to being widely recognized as an important asset to the students, staff, and faculty, and one that continues to play a vital role in the ongoing life of the School. It is still on an upward trajectory towards greater service and new opportunities for alums and students – and through active outreach and involvement, greater service to alumni of Yale overall.

Impact. Consistent with one of the key goals in the strategic plan, the transformed F&ES alumni program has reached out and re-engaged alumni of all vintages, across the country and around the world, with programs and services that make them want to stay involved and remain a vital component in the ongoing life of the School. Alumni are now networking more closely with one another, with current students, and with prospective students, to become an asset to the School and to one another. This re-engagement has been reflected in greater alumni support for the School and its dean, both financially through contributions to the School's annual fund, and through an increasing number and diversity of volunteer activities.

Closer integration of the Graduate & Professional Schools, including F&ES, is a key element of the current AYA strategic plan. The transformed F&ES alumni program has helped open F&ES to the entire university community and AYA through the educational programs developed in conjunction with its quinquennial reunions, and through involvement in the development of the core program for a recent AYA annual assembly. The F&ES alumni program has also raised the profile of AYA programs with F&ES alums, and has strongly encouraged their involvement with the local Yale Clubs and with volunteer activities such as the Yale Day of Service, Yale Service Corps, Bulldogs (domestic and international), and the Yale Career Network.

The F&ES Alumni Association serves the needs of the alumni and supports the work and outreach of the School of Forestry & Environmental Studies itself. The following examples highlight some of the valuable contributions of the Association to the overall mission of the School:

- ❏ Developed an online network to generate summer internships from alumni for students
- ❏ Visited the School individually and as panelists to offer lectures and presentations to enrich student experience
- ❏ Mentored individual students and student interest groups
- ❏ Organized and hosted regional alumni events across the United States and around the globe
- ❏ Assumed leadership roles for the F&ES annual Reunion Weekend
- ❏ Served on the Association of Yale Alumni Board of Governors to create closer ties between F&ES and the greater Yale University community
- ❏ Honored exceptional contributions of alumni, faculty and administrators with Distinguished Alumni and Distinguished Service Awards
- ❏ Developed online and social networking opportunities to enhance communication among alumni and with the School
- ❏ Promoted alumni volunteer community service as leaders in such efforts as the Yale Day of Service

3.4 | SIGs
shared interest groups or affinity groups

Background. Increasingly, Yale graduates are coming together to formulate groups on the basis of a "shared identity" or a "shared interest." Collectively, "shared identity groups" and "shared interest groups" are referred to in shorthand as "SIGs." Many universities refer to them as "affinity groups."

Goals. SIGs provide significant opportunities to foster a greater sense of connection to and engagement between members of the alumni community and Yale. Through events and activities, SIGs serve as ambassadors for Yale, supporting institutional goals and promoting the reputation of the University. SIGs also help to identify talented prospective students, as well as volunteer alumni leaders.

Organizing structure. The Association of Yale Alumni offers SIGs the opportunity for formal recognition which brings about corresponding benefits. To receive official recognition from AYA, SIGs must satisfy the following five criteria: Membership threshold of at least 100 alumni; Volunteer leadership of, at minimum, two officers; Preparation of Articles of Incorporation and By-Laws; Preparation of a three-year strategic plan; and Submission of an annual report. To date, the AYA has recognized a total of 61 SIGs. This number continues to grow.

Benefits. Upon receiving formal AYA recognition, SIGs are granted permission for use of the Yale name. In an effort to help publicize the existence of a SIG, the AYA will include the group name and key information on the AYA website and provide web hosting for the group's own website. AYA will also distribute two start-up broadcast e-mail communications to prospective members and provide updated member lists.

3.4.1 | Sports Associations
connecting to Yale through athletics

Athletics at Yale. In the United States, most universities have amateur sports teams, and participate in university-based sports leagues. In fact in the U.S., much of amateur sports revolves around university sports leagues rather than non-university-based sports clubs. Some students come to Yale as recruited athletes, already very accomplished in their sport of choice. Others try out for teams having little or no prior experience. The best and most committed athletes are selected for varsity and club teams, but opportunities also exist for others through Yale's intramural leagues. Through many hours of hard work toward a shared goal, student athletes build life-long friendships and associations.

Alumni athletic associations. A network of alumni associations represents all of Yale's 35 varsity sports. The associations consist of former athletes, alumni, parents, and friends but membership is open to anyone interested in contributing or getting involved with Yale athletics. Many associations organize annual gatherings that include both current undergraduate athletes and alumni. Associations typically are governed by officers elected from the membership, usually with undergraduate representation.

Activities beget success. Alumni associations communicate information about upcoming games/races/meets and team results to alumni and friends. Through the offering of career networking and job placement, hosting of special events including receptions, alumni/alumnae games, golf outings, and the raising of money to support Yale athletics, associations enhance the experience between Yale and the alumni community. Association fund raising supplements the team budgets and helps cover recruiting costs, team travel, equipment, communications, and other annual team expenses. These contributions provide coaches with the resources necessary to attract the best and the brightest to come to Yale and to be successful scholar athletes.

Creating lasting loyalties. After graduation, athletic associations provide a lasting network for Yale alumni. Job placement and career networking can be extremely valuable, and connections to a particular sport or to Yale athletics in general can open doors across generations. Affiliation with an athletic team gives alumni a more personal and direct connection to Yale. This more focused association can help to elicit donations both to support the team they once played on and to support Yale as a whole. Games, races, and meets provide focal points around which receptions and other gatherings can be organized. Such events help alumni remember and even re-live their happy undergraduate experiences, reinforcing loyalties that might otherwise fade over time.

3.4.2 | Yale Alumni Entrepreneurs

The idea. "Entrepreneurship can be a powerful force for good, in the New Haven community and beyond" the report for Yale Tomorrow concluded.

"The emergence of an entrepreneurial economy is the most significant and hopeful event to have occurred in recent economic and social history" Peter Drucker underscored.

Yale Alumni Entrepreneurs (YAE) is a new alumni group starting in New York and Cleveland with the support of the Association of Yale Alumni in New Haven to seize a historic and untapped opportunity for the University, alumni, students and their communities, worldwide. Specifically, the opportunity is to develop new and successful for profit and nonprofit businesses by connecting start-up entrepreneur Yale alumni with successful entrepreneur Yale alumni and others as free mentors, in each community of participating Yale alumni worldwide.

Emphasizing the new entrepreneurial opportunity for people around the world. YAE is intended to increase young alumni involvement in Yale Alumni associations and other alumni activities, and also create new businesses and income that benefit nonprofit and for profit organizations and people including Yale University, alumni, students, faculty, and their communities around the world.

Organization. YAE is a separate legal entity responsible for the mentoring program made available at participating local Yale alumni associations and for operating a network linked to the AYA, the Yale Entrepreneurial Institute (YEI) which serves Yale students, and other alumni or entrepreneurial groups as appropriate.

How it works. An alumnus submits a short description of the venture idea to YAE locally. An intake alumnus conducts a phone or in person interview to determine what information is needed to flesh out the idea, and, when ready for mentoring, identifies appropriate mentors. A pool of local mentors with various types of industry and subject expertise, including marketing, management, financial and legal, is assembled locally. Each local YAE mentor pool also can draw on YAE and other mentor pools nationally and internationally as it determines.

3.4.3 | The Yale Alumni Chorus
friendships from singing together

The power of song. In 1997, a group of 200 choral singers from 30 states around the United States traveled to China for a two-week tour. The chorus, comprised of Yale alumni and their spouses, children and friends, performed a repertoire of classical and collegiate music that reflected the same music many of the singers had performed when they were undergraduates at Yale University in New Haven, Connecticut (USA).

For the individuals of all ages, ranging from recent graduates, to participants in their 80's, it was a life changing and rejuvenating experience as everyone, both singers in the chorus and those who attended the concerts, recognized the power of musically-based intercultural exchange.

Ambassadors of song. Since the first trip to China in 1997, the Yale Alumni Chorus, or YAC, as it has come to be known, has traveled to over 13 countries on 6 continents. YAC has performed in the State Kremlin Palace, the first American U.S. chorus invited to perform there, participated in an exchange program at Cambridge University in the UK and had tours to South Africa and South America. YAC has a repertoire which includes many folk songs sung in native languages. The Chorus has learned many of these songs in master classes led by musicians in the countries where they are performing.

The Yale Alumni Chorus. In 2003, recognizing the real phenomenon the Chorus had become, it was formally established as The Yale Alumni Chorus Foundation, Inc. and was granted recognition as a 501(c)(3) charitable organization for U.S. tax purposes. The Foundation's Board of Directors sets Foundation Policy and engages in oversight of the entire enterprise to ensure that established policy is followed.

3.4.4 | YaleWomen
creating opportunities for women of Yale

From women at Yale to YaleWomen. Since their admission to Yale College in 1969, women have played an increasingly important role in the life of the University, as students, administrators, faculty, and alumnae. Yale's alumnae from all the schools, currently numbering about 50,000, or one-third of Yale's total alumni body, are engaged in traditional AYA activities, from cultural events, service initiatives and travel, to class, club and professional and shared interest groups – as participants and leaders. Many women are also generous donors to Yale. Recently, alumnae have welcomed the opportunity to focus specifically on women graduates, to engage the potential to connect with each other and with Yale.

A March 2010 conference celebrating the 140th anniversary of women at Yale University and the 40th anniversary of women in Yale College was the galvanizing event for the formation of YaleWomen, an organization for Yale alumnae. The conference showcased the accomplishments of women graduates, and provided more than 300 participants the opportunity to network with each other – a call to action for many.

Local meetings grow to national organization. Initially on a regional basis, women organized get-togethers to make friends and professional connections, and to engage in all the ways Yalies engage. These informal gatherings created a new energy. Many women who had not participated in traditional alumni events attended. This led to a Strategic Planning Retreat in February 2011, and a strategic plan for YaleWomen was created.

Networking and mentorship. Women share ideas and advice: from professional to personal, from climbing up – or climbing off – the corporate ladder, to juggling career and family. One participant noted: "While I can discuss these issues in mixed groups, I prefer to get advice from other women." Similar activities are developing to mentor students and create networks within professions.

Developing meaningful relationships. The organization is still young, but full of energy. It's hard to predict how it will evolve – campus partnerships, service opportunities, fund-raising, professional mentoring … all of these are possible. It may not generate interest from all women graduates, but it's already engaging some alumnae who have not been involved with Yale before.

3.5 | Service Programs and Initiatives

Yale has a long tradition of public service, from its original charter to train young people "for Publick employment both in Church and Civil State" to the student-led community-based programs at Dwight Hall, the umbrella organization for service programs at Yale.

For many alumni, the interest in service started with volunteer-driven community-based programs that they engaged in while at Yale. It extends to the many Yale alumni who engage in life long careers at the highest levels of government service and NGO management. Yale alumni have risen to the challenge to 'change the world,' and indeed many are doing just that as volunteers for Yale, or in their professional lives in the nonprofit sector, or serving on boards of foundations, or as elected officials, or by giving of their intelligence and creative energy to volunteer community projects.

For many alumni, programs that give them the opportunity to change lives with other Yalies, family and friends have re-energized and deepened the connection to alma mater. These types of programs extend engagement with the university beyond the traditional alumni connections that emphasize support for the institution or for the alumni group to serving the local community or an underserved community somewhere else in the world. These programs form strong bonds among the participating alumni from the power of working together to help others.

3.5.1 | Yale Day of Service

The Yale Day of Service. Based on Yale's long tradition of service, the Yale Day of Service began as a pilot program in 2008 in Connecticut and was then implemented globally in 2009. Every year since 2009, the Association of Yale Alumni has designated the second Saturday of May as the Yale Day of Service (YDoS). Alumni volunteer leaders for regional clubs work together with AYA, an alumni Chairperson of YDoS and (alumni) Regional Directors of YDoS – along with shared interest groups, segments of classes and local chapters of professional and graduate school alumni organizations – plan local community service projects for that one day.

YDoS projects range from helping to paint a community day care to serving food at soup kitchens for the poor, from cleaning trash out of a local stream to preparing food packages for the needy at local food banks, and much more. Each project has a volunteer coordinator to manage those who register to participate at that site. Sometimes a group of Yale alumni will organize their own special project. In 2014, the Day of Service involved 4000 members of the Yale community volunteering in over 250 sites in 40 states and 20 countries. On the Day of Service, alumni all over the world come together, with family, friends, and neighbors – separately and as Yale united – through the common act of providing service to others.

A Benefit to Clubs. Perhaps one of the most interesting outcomes is the way in which it has appealed to so many alumni who had never before participated in Yale alumni activities. This program can help to bring new energy to local Yale clubs by attracting alumni who have not previously been engaged with Yale or their local Yale Clubs. And, by bringing in new people as part of the YDoS planning process, additional volunteer leadership can be developed for local clubs.

A Benefit to Yale. Participation in the Day of Service reconnects many alumni to Yale – many who were not otherwise engaged in alumni programs. It also introduces many communities to Yale, or at least to another side of Yale. This promotes a positive image of Yale and its support for local communities which in turn enhances its ability to attract the best and brightest students.

3.5.2 | Yale Alumni Service Corps

Changing lives through service work around the world. The Yale Alumni Service Corps (YASC) is a strategic initiative of the Association of Yale Alumni that promotes mutual cross-cultural awareness and sustainable development in underserved communities. YASC does this by bringing Yale alumni, family and friends together to work with people in communities throughout the world – bringing introduction to the arts, creative education and new sports, offering public health, and economic development – to inspire hope and produce meaningful change in the lives of the people it serves.

Geography of programs. Programs have been successfully carried out in the Dominican Republic, Mexico, Brazil, China, Nicaragua, Ghana, and India. YASC has partnered with College Summit for college mentoring programs in West Virginia, Upstate New York and California.

Learning about others through cultural exchange is a valuable part of the program. YASC participants learn through teaching English, dance, music, math, painting and computers, building playgrounds and libraries, coaching soccer and baseball, conducting medical clinics, providing health education, visits to private houses, and offering small business consulting for local entrepreneurs and farmers.

Enduring impact occurs as YASC partners with local universities and other service organizations to enrich programs and ensure volunteers share their skills with community leaders, local health care workers and students to promote self-sufficiency and sustainability.

3.5.3 | Yale Global Alumni Leadership Exchange connecting Yale to the world

The internationalization of Yale. Twenty-first century Yale strives to be a global university. Under the leadership of President Peter Salovey, Yale seeks to attract students and faculty from around the world, share and adopt best practices from abroad, and exchange initiatives with leading educational institutions of other nations. The Association of Yale Alumni complements these efforts through YaleGALE (Yale Alumni Leadership Exchange).

The changing role of alumni. At Yale, as at many institutions of higher education in the United States, alumni volunteers play a significant part in the life of the institution. They recruit students, employ graduates, provide social and volunteer opportunities, promote the institution, and provide philanthropic support. In other countries and cultures, alumni have taken different paths to become involved with their universities, particularly regarding admissions, alumni relations, and fundraising. The AYA has much to learn from its counterparts abroad, and much to share.

The YaleGALE program. YaleGALE partners with leading universities to conduct alumni leadership exchanges around the world. Delegations of 25-60 Yale alumni, who have served as volunteer leaders in AYA, travel with their families to host countries where they share ideas on alumni relations in conferences, seminars and workshops. They also visit significant cultural landmarks and institutions, and build lasting friendships between Yale alumni and alumni leaders of premiere global higher education institutions.

Most YaleGALE participants have been active for years in various AYA programs at the regional or national level. Many have been members of the AYA Board of Governors. For YaleGALE, participant volunteers create events, prepare presentations, write promotional materials, develop itineraries and maintain relationships with partner universities.

Why do Yale alumni participate? Yale alumni participants volunteer their own time and pay their own way to participate in a YaleGALE exchange. They do it to give back, because Yale has given them so much – so much more than just an education. At Yale, they have learned, taken to heart, and enriched their lives with ideals of service to others. They have gained lifelong friends, and sometimes even spouses or partners. For these leaders Yale is family – and participating in a YaleGALE event deepens these family ties.

3.6 | Student-Alumni Initiatives

Our goal. *To Connect the Yale Generations – Past & Present.* What happens when Yale brings together its students and alumni? Yale students and alumni form dynamic relationships that benefit both groups. Yale students fill alumni with energy, showing them what campus life is like today, and draw them back to campus – and into Yale service, sometimes for the first time since they graduated. Interacting with Yale alumni allows current students to receive valuable career advice and guidance on how to adjust to life after graduation. Students also form ties to the Association of Yale Alumni even before they graduate. Yale's traditions and values are exchanged between the Yale generations, as students and alumni form meaningful connections and lasting friendships.

Our structure. *The Student-Alumni Initiatives Committee.* What is the Student-Alumni Initiatives Committee? It is a working committee of the AYA Board of Governors that creates programs to connect Yale's alumni and current Yale students. Our committee consists of ten volunteer board members that meet in person four times a year and via telephone every month. The programs we develop are based on the input we receive from student and alumni interviews, surveys and group discussions.

Our programs. *Creating Connection Points for Students & Alumni.* We work in partnership with student groups to develop and host a variety of relevant student-alumni programs throughout the year. These include: sponsoring alumni speaker panels where alumni share career advice about different fields (e.g., careers in medicine, academia, law, etc.); delivering speeches to students to educate them about AYA programs and how to get involved; and hosting receptions and lunches for students and alumni to network and exchange ideas.

Our future. *Creating Students & Alumni at Yale (STAY).* How do we make these student-alumni connections endure? We are currently establishing Students and Alumni at Yale, a permanent shared interest group, which will be made-up of a group of current and recently graduated students, alumni board members and other interested alumni. Expanding the leadership of this group will allow for membership continuity over time. STAY will continue to create programs that change student and alumni lives and Yale, forever.

AYA and University Career Services is building a new program to bring student and alumni together to prepare students for life beyond the campus. The program is intended to provide life-skills support as well as career guidance for students.

Chapter 4

Undergraduate Admissions and alumni volunteers

In some countries, admission to university, college, or institute may depend primarily on a prospective student's score on a nation-wide test. In contrast, admissions at most American universities is more holistic, relating not only to scores on nation-wide tests (SATs/ACTs), but also high school grades, extra-curricular activities and essays. Some, such as Yale, also rely on interviews with prospective students – given mostly by alumni volunteers.

4.1 | Admission to Yale and alumni interviewing

The role of interviewing in admission to Yale. Yale has long considered interviews with prospective undergraduate students to be helpful in the application process. Like many colleges and universities in the United States, Yale does not consider standardized test scores exclusively when making admissions decisions. Yale also considers high school grades, leadership potential, academic ranking, extra- curricular activities, special talents, student motivation, and a variety of other factors. While these factors may be difficult to compare, an interview with the applicant can help put them in perspective.

Many applicants, however, live far from Yale, and not every applicant is able to visit. In addition, Yale just does not have sufficient staff to interview the almost 30,000 students who apply every year. For that reason, Yale does not require an interview. But believing in the interview's importance, Yale relies on alumni volunteers around the country and around the world to interview students in their home towns.

The role of the Alumni Schools Committee. The Yale Alumni Schools Committee consists of Yale alumni devoted to the interviewing of students applying to Yale. Historically, 65% of the students applying to Yale receive a one-on-one interview with an alumnus or alumna. The alumnus or alumna conducting the interview writes a one-page report to the Admissions Office answering the following four questions:

❑ To what extent will the applicant contribute to the Yale community?

❑ To what extent will the applicant benefit from the Yale community?

❑ To what extent does the applicant pursue his or her interests?

❑ To what extent does the applicant make sacrifices to pursue his or her interests?

The benefit of the interview to the applicant. The interview is 60 to 90 minutes long and can be used as a two-way street, with the interviewer providing the applicant with information about Yale while at the same time obtaining information from the applicant for his report. This turns the interview into a conversation, rather than a trial, enabling the applicant to show his or her personality more comfortably. Finally, while the interview is intended to be private, the interviewer may invite the applicant's parents to have their questions answered, particularly about financial aid.

The benefit to the alumni. The Alumni Schools Committee is one of the most popular ways for alumni to participate in the life of the University. Applicants often remember the alumni interviewers – and remember how the interaction with that person helped him or her choose Yale.

A benefit to Yale. Often, the alumni interview is the only direct personal contact between Yale and the applicant, since not all applicants are able to travel to New Haven and staff time at the admissions office is limited. The report may be particularly useful where the admissions office is trying to decide between two equally qualified candidates.

4.2 | The Admissions Office and the Alumni Schools Network

The role of outreach in admission to Yale. Yale offers students a world class education. However, many promising students do not consider Yale because it seems so far from their home town, or because none of their friends and classmates are applying. Others believe they cannot afford to attend Yale, because they are not aware of the extraordinary amount of financial aid that Yale makes available. To address this, the staff of the Admissions Office holds information sessions in most regions of the United States. However, a prospective applicant who has dismissed Yale as a possibility is not likely to attend an information session. Consequently, Yale relies on dedicated alumni volunteers to spread the word about Yale's accessibility and affordability.

The role of the Alumni Schools Network. The Alumni Schools Network functions as a subcommittee of the Alumni Schools Committee and consists of members of the Alumni Schools Committee who are particularly devoted to interviewing students and who by personality and predilection will be helpful in visiting students at local high schools in September and October.

The objective of these visits is not to recruit, but rather to make information about Yale available to students, so that they may make informed judgments about the prospect of applying to Yale. These visits are coordinated with the Admissions Office at Yale and with guidance counselors at the school. Guidance counselors are a good source of information about the students, particularly the juniors who are likely candidates for Yale in the following year.

The benefit to Yale. The interviewer thus becomes a kind of ambassador for Yale, helping to find the right "fit" between Yale and the student. Viewing his task in this manner, the interviewer is less likely to become "vested" in his judgment about any one interviewee and less likely to be disappointed if any particular interviewee is not admitted.

The benefit to the alumni. This role of "ambassador" allows alumni to communicate their love of Yale, and their love of learning, to the next generation. It also increases their commitment to Yale.

The Alumni Schools Network works to the advantage of students, high schools, Alumni Schools Committee interviewers and Yale by systematizing the process of encouraging the best and brightest students to apply to Yale.

4.3 | Yale Alumni Schools Ambassadors

Yale Alumni Schools Ambassadors (YASA) is a pioneering initiative built on the passion and dedication of Admissions volunteers – giving them the opportunity to serve abroad as ambassadors for Yale, the liberal arts, and the U.S. college experience.

YASA volunteers will travel to areas identified by our Office of Admissions to educate young people about the idea of a liberal arts education, and why coming to the U.S. to attend college could be an extraordinary opportunity.

The inaugural alumni delegation in 2015 focused on one particularly under-resourced area identified by the Admissions Office – the Balkans – with visits to Albania, Bosnia and Macedonia. There were 40 delegates ranging from the Class of '17 to the Class of '57. There were also participants from School of Management (SOM), the Law School and the School of Public Health. Friends and family were full participants in the mission of the trip as they too shared their college experiences and how a liberal arts education helped them in their careers.

During the trip, YASA conducted seven conferences for students, parents, and school administrators to meet with YASA participants. Discussion topics and sessions included Liberal Arts Curriculum, College Fair Information, Career Advice, College Living in the U.S., the Application Process, Financial Aid Information, How to Interview, and Essay review. The group worked with over 650 students during a ten day trip.

Chapter 5

Giving at Yale: the Yale Office of Development and the Yale Alumni Fund

At Yale, the most prominent fundraising efforts are those administered through the Office of Development. These include the annual giving campaigns run by the Yale Alumni Fund as well as larger multi-year capital campaigns. These efforts are detailed below. In addition Classes, Clubs, individual Graduate and Professional Schools alumni groups, as well as individual Shared Interest Groups may have their own (and usually more limited) fundraising efforts.

5.1 | Annual Giving through the Yale Alumni Fund

Annual giving to support Yale. The Yale Alumni Fund is the University's annual giving program, through which the Office of Development – charged with fundraising for the University – solicits gifts from 150,000 alumni on an annual basis. While alumni might make special capital gifts during a Class Reunion or during a Campaign, the University's goal for the Alumni Fund is to encourage alumni to make a gift every year to support the University's core operations.

Annual giving provides the University a vital, steady stream of funds and an opportunity to cultivate and sustain relationships with alumni which may lead to significant future gifts. The Alumni Fund priorities are to connect with every alumnus to provide a vehicle for supporting Yale; to raise unrestricted funds for budget relief; and to grow leadership annual giving (gifts of $1,000 to $100,000).

The Alumni Fund Team. More than 2,000 alumni are directly involved in soliciting their peers for annual gifts. Volunteer leadership is a key element of any successful fundraising program. Peer solicitation is a very effective way to ask alumni for gifts, since a request from a classmate can be particularly motivating. In 2013-14, Alumni Fund staff and volunteers sent over 1,500,000 mail and email solicitations and made over 50,000 telephone calls. These efforts generated record results – the Alumni Fund raised $35.2 million in unrestricted gifts from 44,462 alumni and parents. The average gift to the Fund in 2013-14 was $791.

Every year, right from the beginning! Even while students are on campus they begin to hear about annual giving and participate as the newest alumni in giving back to Yale. The Yale College Senior Class Gift program teaches students about the impact of alumni giving. Classmates who volunteer to ask their friends to make a gift receive training, tools and networking opportunities to learn from experienced alumni volunteers. In 2014, 97% of the Senior Class contributed, raising over $33,000 from classmates, and triggering over $275,000 in challenge gifts, for a total of more than $308,000!

Reunions: gathering, and giving back. Every year, about 15,000 Yale College alumni celebrate a reunion. Many come back to campus to see friends, and many also recognize their reunion by making a special gift, often working with a volunteer from their class on the Reunion Gift Committee or the Alumni Fund, and Development staff.

5.2 | Capital Campaign Fundraising at Yale

The role of charitable giving. Charitable giving is vital to the long-term health of the university. Yale is fortunate to have so many generous, engaged individuals who provide financial support for ongoing educational initiatives, research, facilities, extracurricular activities, and new programs. Funds raised by the Yale Development office may be available for immediate use, or invested in the Yale endowment, which had grown to $16.6 billion in 2010. But endowment growth depends not only upon investment gains but also upon ongoing gifts. In 1950, Yale's endowment was valued at $132 million. If donors did not continue to make subsequent gifts, in 2010 the endowment would have grown to less than $5 billion.

Yale Tomorrow. The "Yale Tomorrow" campaign was a focused, multi-year effort to inspire significant philanthropic support from alumni, parents, friends, corporations and foundations for these campaign priorities: Yale College, the Arts at Yale, the Sciences at Yale, and Yale and the World. The campaign exceeded its goal of $3.5 billion and concluded on June 30, 2011.

Who gives? Who makes gifts to Yale? While there are many sources of support – alumni, parents, friends, foundations and corporations – over 63% of the funds raised for Yale Tomorrow came from alumni. Relationships with donors are built over time and tend to follow a cycle: from identification, to interest, to involvement, to investment, to stewardship. There is a ladder of philanthropic support: from individuals, from first-time donors, to renewals, to annual unrestricted gifts, to major/capital gifts, to planned gifts (life income or bequests). Typically the gifts at the top of the ladder are larger, more complex, and require personal contact.

Why alumni give. Alumni have very personal reasons for giving to Yale. Donors often cite their educational experience, relationships, activities, history, residential colleges, and financial aid (particularly if alumni received aid when they were students themselves) as reasons they give. Each gift is a demonstration of the passion that Yale alumni feel for their alma mater.

Every gift matters. Gifts to Yale at all levels make a difference. Large capital gifts may have transformational impact. One such contribution is the gift by Edward Harkness, Yale College Class of 1897, which established the residential colleges that serve as the hub of undergraduate life today. Annual giving at more modest levels promotes participation and demonstrates the breadth of philanthropic support by alumni.

 **PART II**

THE PROCESS OF ORGANIZING VOLUNTEER COMMUNITIES

This part of the Guide focuses on working with volunteers. It will examine finding and engaging volunteers, as well as cultivating them and helping them develop into leaders. It will address helping them organize into effective working groups, as well as creating organizations within which volunteers can flourish. It will consider nurturing values in your institution which will develop a culture of loyalty that encourages volunteering, as well as providing effective communication channels to and among your volunteers.

But the big question many ask is, "Why should you work with volunteers, when after all, professionals are so much more ... professional?" Because volunteers bring much more to their efforts than their time and their talents – they bring loyalty, gratitude, and passion. These are the reasons a volunteer works with you. These are the reasons you want their help.

Alumni wanting to give back as volunteers have been responsible for starting most alumni programs – because they are passionate and driven. These people care and they want to give back because they are grateful for what they received and they appreciate being part of a community. They want to keep the institution, its alumni, and other volunteers engaged and connected. Volunteers are often the key element in keeping the institution entrepreneurial especially for a large organization.

No matter what you seek from alumni – whether to serve the community, to provide programming for each other, to advise the institution, or to give money – most alumni relate to each other based on shared experiences and shared values which is inspiring at a deep and meaningful level. Even alumni who give money but do not volunteer are inspired by the time and talent given by alumni volunteers.

Just as importantly – you must reward your volunteers – with respect and loyalty and gratitude. This thread runs throughout the Guide. The more you thank those who give time, talent, or treasure, the more you will attract new volunteers that understand the power and rewards of volunteering.

Effectively supporting and rewarding volunteers includes listening to them, giving them ownership of their projects, training them, backing them up, helping them realize their goals and passions, providing organization so that they can accomplish what they want, and thanking them. There are many ways to convey the spirit of this message, and this Guide will do it often.

Remember, to work effectively with volunteers, it's not about you – it's about enabling them.

Chapter 6

Developing Volunteers and Volunteer Leaders

Volunteering is an integral part of many organizations. Often, this is not just for budgetary reasons, but also for philosophical ones reaching down to the organization's core mission and vision. When volunteering is key, finding volunteers and maintaining their dedication and commitment are a necessity.

6.1 | Volunteer Engagement
recruiting and retaining volunteers

Volunteers are essential for almost every not-for-profit organization, NGO, and community support association including most educational institutions. The volunteer is someone who cares enough to devote personal time and often money to advance your organization's mission. Volunteers are often the best candidates to perform important tasks, spread the word about your mission, and connect your organization with the larger body of people you want to reach even if you have an unlimited budget. A good and committed volunteer will enthusiastically and capably take on work that you cannot afford to pay anyone else to do.

Volunteers expand the capacity of professional staff and the organization to fulfill its mission. They can be your best ambassadors, telling others about your organization and encouraging additional support of all kinds. They know people you don't know. They also provide insight about the preferences and evolving culture of the larger community. A university uses its volunteers to do some very different things than does a social service organization. Identify the right opportunities for volunteers in your organization and welcome them into participating in your important work.

Why would someone volunteer to support your organization with time and energy? Volunteers have to understand and care about your mission. A person will volunteer when passionate about what your organization stands for and does. While they may receive social benefits, volunteers help because they believe that the organization and the work they do for the organization are important and meaningful.

Recruiting volunteers. Recruiting volunteers requires thought, planning and coordination. Volunteers need to know what is expected of them: what they will do, how much time it will take and what impact their efforts will have. Organized volunteers are happy volunteers. Some volunteers will prefer to take on certain types of responsibilities and may be uncomfortable if asked to perform others.

Recruit volunteers enthusiastically. Be prepared to tell potential volunteers how much they will enjoy participating with your wonderful organization, what they will help accomplish and why they will find it meaningful. Encourage volunteers to share their passion and recruit their friends.

Know what you need them to do. When people ask, you should be able to tell them what is needed and what the responsibilities will be – will they be advising on an existing effort or creating a new one? Will they be asked to work on social media or to write articles? Organize the activity so volunteers are not wasting their time.

Anticipate who is likely to offer to help. Students? Retired people? Families? Do your best to match individuals and their preferred tasks so as to keep them engaged and happy. For example, a terrific event organizer might be a poor fundraiser.

Managing volunteers. Volunteers are there because they want to be, and generally they will stay as long as the work and the environment are satisfying. And some volunteers will leave the organization no matter what you do. That is why any organization that uses volunteers needs to allocate significant professional time to managing volunteers. In a purely volunteer organization, the (volunteer) leadership needs to manage recruitment and cultivation of new volunteers and new leadership. Good volunteer management can facilitate effective long term engagement and reduce the number of volunteers who lose interest and then leave.

Plan professional time to oversee volunteer activity. Volunteers need to be engaged with the professionals in the organization and feel that they are an integral part of the organization's work. Also, the organization should arrange for volunteers to socialize with each other. Making new friends reinforces their loyalty.

Manage them to do what is asked. This is similar to managing an employee. A volunteer role is a responsibility like a job. Be sure to give them tasks they can do well and find rewarding.

Watch for potential leaders. If you are looking for volunteer leaders, be prepared to ask individuals who show competence to take on a larger role with more responsibility.

Thank them. Then thank them again. And again. About 25% of volunteer management is thanking people. Volunteers who work at a distance or only part time are easy to take for granted. Acknowledging them repeatedly works wonders in keeping them engaged.

6.2 | The 40th Reunion of the Class of 1970 a case study in volunteer engagement

While there are many facets to any reunion, homecoming, or special event, this Case Study will look at what the Class of 1970 Reunion planners – including alumni volunteers, the Association of Yale Alumni reunion staff, and AYA itself – did to recruit, motivate, retain, and recognize volunteers for that reunion. (Note: Yale and American universities, in general, denote Classes by the year of graduation, rather than the year of matriculation. Also, AYA uses the term Classes to refer to cohorts graduating from Yale College, not the graduate and professional schools.)

This Case Study presents the 40th Reunion of the Yale Class of 1970 because it received the Outstanding Class Award for programming and excellence in 2010, the year AYA instituted several Awards to recognize alumni volunteer efforts and programming excellence.

Background. *Yale Classes began having reunions almost two centuries ago,* starting when Yale was almost exclusively an undergraduate college. The Class of 1821 held the first Yale Class Reunion in 1824. At that time the graduating Class had only about 70 members – and Class members did all the planning and organizing of the Reunion.

But times have changed. Classes are larger and people live longer – and more groupings of alumni hold reunions, homecomings and special events. So in any one year there are more reunions in total (including reunions for the graduate and professional schools as well as shared interest and identity groups), more Class reunions and more people coming to all of them. Now, a Yale College Class includes about 1350 students – though that will increase about 15% when Yale finishes building the two new residential colleges. Each Class has a reunion every 5 years so each year thirteen classes hold a reunion back at Yale. These thirteen reunions bring 7000 alumni, family and friends to campus in late spring every year. Officially, each Class reunion starts on Thursday or Friday and ends on Sunday. Some alumni come for only one day, and some come for only one dinner. Many stay on-Campus, in student housing.

Seven thousand visiting party-goers are more people than the Yale Campus can accommodate at one time. Consequently the reunions have to be held after graduation ceremonies when most students have left Campus, and they have to be held over two consecutive weekends in late May or early June. To create venues for the festivities, the AYA erects 8 large high-top tents around campus – each of which provides dinner space for hundreds of people. And during each of these weekends approximately 3500 alumni, family and friends descend upon New Haven.

Today, the dining, lodging, serving, entertaining, venue tents, sound systems, security, and co-ordination of all reunion events require professional management and a budget of millions of dollars. In general, the AYA pays for those reunion activities with funds generated by attendance fees, a general fund and subsidized by class treasury subsidies (maintained by annual dues) for class-specific activities and meals.

The Association of Yale Alumni currently employs a staff of 7 whose primary duty is to work with Classes on their programs and projects, particularly their reunions. (AYA total staff is approximately 35.) Five staff members are each specifically responsible for 2 to 4 reunions each year. But during the reunions the entire AYA staff is involved.

The AYA has been doing this for a long time, and has kept voluminous records and statistics. For example, it knows the average turnout for a 20th reunion, and how that differs from the average turnout for a 40th reunion. It knows whether the reunion attendance for a particular Class is above or below the average for all Classes for that reunion. For the 40th Reunion of the Class of 1970, AYA estimated (9 months in advance) that 254 alumni would return, bringing 178 guests. The actual numbers were 251 alumni and 168 guests.

Clearly, AYA professional staffers could produce a wonderful and successful Class reunion without alumni volunteers from that Class – or with minimal input from them. In rare cases, when Class officers are not active or engaged, the AYA staff has to do so. It is also clear that the AYA professional staff spends considerable time training, coaching, encouraging, managing, and placating alumni volunteers. *However, it is the experience at Yale that the quantity and quality of Class volunteer involvement affects not just reunion attendance, but the attendees' enthusiasm, enjoyment and sense of being a part of the Yale family.*

How do Yale and AYA recruit, train, manage, and thank reunion volunteers? There is much that AYA and Yale do to produce each reunion, but this will focus on its efforts with respect to volunteer engagement.

AYA encourages each Class to choose a volunteer Reunion Chair or Chairs early – more than a year before the reunion event.

AYA provides incentives for a Reunion Chair to start planning a year early – by hosting the Reunion Chair at a reunion of another Class – the year before the Chair's upcoming reunion. This allows the Chair to observe a reunion and how it is managed.

AYA holds a day-long training workshop for all Reunion Chairs at Yale in September, about 9 months before the reunions. Again this is at no cost to any volunteer Chair. The workshop tries to ease the organizational burden on the Chair by providing seminars on (and a 180 page guidebook about) suggested timelines, to-do items, budgets, souvenirs, musicians, entertainers, menus, programs, attendance building letters, etc. A buffet lunch and dinner lets the Chair taste from many of the suggested menus. Handouts include a list of classmates who are potential reunion volunteers because they had each volunteered for other major AYA activities. The training and materials stress that this is a team effort.

❑ Volunteers, or a committee of volunteers, can be recruited for each major task.

❑ It is vital to have an attendance committee of class volunteers, who are willing to contact each classmate individually by letter or phone.

❑ The event must be inclusive, and reaching out to shared interest groups and collectivities within the Class, whether officially SIGs or not, is important.

❑ It is important to work with the Reunion Gift Committee, even though the Reunion Gift Committee is a fundraising component composed of a different set of volunteers under the direction of Yale's Office of Development, rather than the AYA.

During the run-up to the reunion, the AYA staff liaison for the Class gently reminds the Reunion Chair of tasks to do and volunteers to be recruited and managed. AYA and its campus partners are also responsible for finalizing many different logistical aspects of the reunion, such as the meals, transportation, campus housing, audio visual requests, space for class panels, etc.

AYA urges the Reunion Chair (and Reunion Committees) to go for attendance records – and to go beyond the numbers. That is now institutionalized as part of the AYA Excellence Awards which recognize extra-ordinary Class efforts in five different categories (*http://aya.yale. edu/content/award-categories*), posting winners online and describing those efforts for future reference: *https://docs.google.com/file/d/0B_ xST13LJbZ_UXVpUmxTcTlYMUE/edit* .

❑ **Outstanding Class Award.** For the class that exhibits overall excellence in programming, including a successful mix of educational, cultural, athletic, social, and community service programming

❑ **Outstanding BOLD Class Award.** For the "Bulldogs of the Last Decade" class that exhibits excellence in young alumni engagement, either through an array of programming (educational, cultural, athletic, social, and/or community service), a specific initiative, or creative outreach connecting with classmates across the globe

❑ **Highest Reunion Attendance Award.** For highest attendance, measured as total number of alumni, family, and friends attending a quinquennial reunion, and measured against previous reunions of the same anniversary

❑ **Highest Percentage of Returning Alumni Reunion Award.** For highest percentage of returning alumni measured against total living alumni of the class and against previous reunions of the same anniversary

❑ **Outstanding Class Volunteer Engagement and Leadership Award.** For the class that best demonstrates meaningful leadership in strategic planning, volunteer recruitment, financial management, and stewardship

What the Class of 1970 did to recruit, excite, and manage volunteers. One task was keeping the regulars happy. This meant finding volunteers and working with them to accomplish the many things expected of any Yale reunion and expected in particular from past Class of 1970 Reunions. A second task was to do new things in new ways that would actively involve more members of the Class of 1970 in this Reunion – including some who had not previously been involved. This meant empowering volunteers, finding additional ones, and collaborating with others in the University and outside the Class. These efforts started with a handful of classmates: the Chair recruited some of his friends to help, others volunteered themselves, because they wanted to ensure that the reunion had certain programming.

(Much focus for this Reunion was placed on recruiting volunteers who would do or lead things at the Reunion itself. Another way to involve volunteers is to build a very large, inclusive, and extensive attendance committee – for which volunteers contact classmates and friends personally. See for example the 25th Reunion of the Class of 1988, which won the AYA Outstanding Class Award in 2013: *https:// docs.google.com/file/d/0B_xST13LJbZ_UXVpUmxTcTlYMUE/edit* .)

Plans for ensuring a solid foundation and perpetuating Class traditions. The usual type of activities for the regulars.

- ❑ Entertainment Committee to find music (rock and roll bands made up of classmates) for Friday night and Saturday night, and schedule a short concert by classmates who had been in the Whiffenpoofs (senior male a cappella singing group) as students.

- ❑ Programming Committee to find speakers and assemble discussion panels to fill four time slots (2 on Friday afternoon and 2 on Saturday afternoon). Preferably many of the panelists would be classmates.

- ❑ Food Chair to choose from among the AYA proffered menus for the weekend, with a goal of satisfying classmates' differing tastes in food and beverage while containing costs.

- ❑ Attendance Committee to contact as many classmates personally to urge them to attend.

- ❑ Memorial Service organizer to schedule and prepare a memorial service for classmates who had died since the last reunion

- ❑ Art "committee", work with 2 artists who were classmates and had been active volunteers at previous reunions, to produce a reunion logo and decorative artwork

- ❑ Souvenir, arrange production of a memorable souvenir to take home from the reunion.

- ❑ Reunion Book Committee Chair, produce a book with reflections from classmates.

Additional Efforts Requiring New Volunteers. New ideas and initiatives.

- ❑ Entertainment Committee Chair found extra time slots on Friday and Saturday for almost as many Class musicians as volunteered to perform: 38 musicians playing classical, protest, folk, rock, blues, jug band, and jazz participated. Some had never come to a reunion before. Thursday evening featured an iPod playlist of rock 'n' roll from the Class' college years put together by a classmate who was a musician and radio station music announcer during college. In addition, pre-reunion concerts were held in 3 cities.

❑ Programming Committee put together 8 panel discussions for Friday and Saturday (involving 23 classmates) plus a speaker, then found time slots on Thursday for another speaker and another panel.

❑ Food committee was able to save enough money on the weekend meals, to include a free Thursday evening reception.

❑ Art Committee Chair put together a glossy art book of representative work of 17 classmates who worked in the visual arts, and held a book signing at the reunion. This Art Book is in addition to the Reunion Book of reflections listed above. An illustrated self-guided walking tour of notable Yale Campus architecture was also produced by another classmate.

❑ Souvenir, three additional souvenirs were produced in limited quantities to promote pre-reunion events and induce classmates to write reflections for the Reunion Book. (Submit a reflection and get a souvenir.)

❑ Sport Interest Groups. Although some of the biggest undergraduate sports associations (football and swimming) have frequently held all-Class receptions during Reunion weekend, many others had not. For this reunion, Class of 1970 volunteers worked with the Alumni Sports Associations and the Yale Athletic department to hold all-Class receptions for fencing, sailing, and crew – and a pre-reunion fly fishing event at the Yale Pond. For Class members, events featuring martial arts, yoga, and golf were also included.

Not all efforts were successful, but all volunteers (and most classmates) felt more a part of the Reunion.

❑ One classmate proposed a 100 mile long-distance bicycle ride ending at Reunion. Although no one offered to join him, he did make the 100 mile ride.

❑ One volunteer proposed a pre-reunion race-car driving school. A few classmates were interested (and even paid deposits), but not enough to make it work.

THE YaleGALE GUIDE

Not counting contributions either to the Art Book or the Reunion Book, over 60 of the 254 classmates who attended the reunion volunteered their time or services to make it happen. Over 80 contributed to the Art Book and the Reunion Book (some to both).

Most volunteers and many other classmates felt more a part of the Reunion than previously.

What the Class of 1970 did to thank volunteers.

❑ Reunion and pre-reunion activities were featured in the Class blog, along with thanks to volunteers involved in some specific events.

❑ Two emails were sent after the reunion, thanking all volunteers, with copies posted to the Class website: Matters of Note at *http://alumninet.yale.edu/classes/yc1970/40th-note.html* and Plethora of Thanks at *http://alumninet.yale.edu/classes/yc1970/40th-thanks.html* .

Chapter 7

Leadership Cultivation

Voluntary associations and not-for-profit organizations often need leaders who are themselves volunteers. It may be someone to chair an advisory board, lead a team project, or run the whole organization. Finding good leaders, or more accurately training and mentoring them, is no small task for any organization. There are special considerations for a voluntary one. Attention needs to be paid to how leadership is identified, supported, and rewarded, and how the organization is structured to facilitate cultivating volunteer leadership.

7.1 | Nurturing Leaders

Volunteer leaders are the lifeblood of a successful alumni association. They serve the functional role of being a staff multiplier – they are on the ground, all over the world, with the potential to use their time, talents and treasure to represent the organization and advance its interests.

Volunteer leaders are like other leaders. So, many aspects of nurturing leaders are similar in any organization.

Identifying basic talent, competency and management ability of potential leaders is similar for volunteer-led organizations as it is for other organizations. **Training** people, **teaching** them and providing **mentoring** involve many of the same processes and skill sets. See *www.handsonnetwork.org/files/resources/BP_VolunteerRecruitment_2010_HON.pdf* for recruiting volunteers. For recruiting volunteer leaders see: *www.handsonnetwork.org/files/resources/GI_DevelopingVolunteerLeaders_2010_HON.pdf* .

But some aspects of nurturing volunteer leaders are not like nurturing other leaders.

How are volunteer organizations different? Your volunteers are not working for a paycheck. They are volunteers, not employees. So, if you treat your volunteers poorly, they can leave – and will. It is important to realize that your volunteers receive non-monetary compensation largely in the form of respect and gratitude. They receive additional compensation in the form of the training they receive – both for specific jobs and for leadership training – and the experience. For some, the contacts and networking may serve as compensation. Volunteers also receive gratification by feeling that they have done something important, and have done it well. This is why it is essential to treat volunteers with respect including showing appreciation for their efforts.

Not everything always goes smoothly when working with volunteers any more than it does in a corporate setting. Sometimes a volunteer is not suited to a role or to a task which creates a situation that needs careful and tactful handling. It is possible to redirect volunteer enthusiasm and, if necessary, counsel out a volunteer who either is ineffective, not working well with others, or may no longer act in alignment with the mission of the organization. Ideally, by knowing your volunteers well, it is possible to prevent some of the problems but not all.

The most important words are "thank you". Good leaders know how to thank and recognize people. Recognition of volunteers is of paramount importance in volunteer organizations because it can be the currency for volunteer motivation. For Nine Rules of Recognition, see *http://www.handsonnetwork.org/files/resources/The_Nine_Rules_of_Recognition.pdf* .

❑ **Give people real and meaningful jobs.** Jobs that are within their capabilities. This means explaining why even drudge jobs are important to the organization. And thank them, especially for doing the thankless jobs.

❑ **Train your people to do the jobs well.** If you want volunteers to do the job as well as employees, you have to train them just as well – they deserve it and your organizational success requires it.

❏ **Give your people opportunities to take on more challenging and difficult work.** And thank them for taking on the added responsibility.

❏ **Mentor them, support them and watch their back.** This includes warning your people about potential obstacles, suggesting ways to deal with those obstacles, and sometimes using your own influence to smooth the way. This is so that the people you mentor can grow into these greater responsibilities, succeed at them, and want to take on even more.

❏ **Give your people a voice.** Giving people more responsibilities includes bringing them into the decision making process -- at a level appropriate to their skills – and taking their comments respectfully and seriously. Thank them for their comments, even if you don't adopt them.

❏ **Bring them to meetings.** Introduce them to organization leaders and the public when appropriate. This allows your people's value to be seen, appreciated, and acknowledged by others.

Manage Volunteer Burnout. Managing burnout starts from day one. Components include support, supervision, engagement and recognition. For more see *http://www.handsonnetwork.org/files/resources/volunteer_burnout_.pdf* .

Mentoring Caveats. Nurturing new leaders requires mentoring them. Here are some things to remember.

❏ **The people you mentor will never be exactly like you**. They will do things differently. You have to let them.

❏ **People learn by making mistakes.** Supervision and autonomy need to be balanced. Give people the opportunity to fail. Then help them fix mistakes, and teach them to learn from them.

❏ **A well-mentored person will outgrow the job.** The leaders you nurture will want to be leaders themselves. When the time comes, help them find another organization to lead or step aside.

7.2 | Publicly Recognizing Volunteers through awards

Thanking volunteers is necessary. It is the right thing to do. It is motivating and inspiring for the volunteer and for other volunteers and it nurtures leadership potential. Showing appreciation can take many forms, from a simple spoken (and heartfelt) thank you to spoken public recognition at gatherings, from tangible gifts to more permanent forms such as engraved on-site plaques. One method of public recognition involves giving awards.

The way that the award is presented is as important at the award itself. Both have to be geared to the value, importance and nature of the acts that are being rewarded. Contributions of time and talent need appropriate recognition just as much as large contributions of money that often result in naming something after the donor (such as a building, a professorship, a scholarship, etc.) – after all Yale was named after its first large donor.

Below are some examples of recognition for volunteer and alumni service bestowed by Yale. Each example lists **what is given, for what it is given, who decides** to give it, **who presents** the award, and in **what setting.** There is great variety in these examples, which show some of the ways in which recognition can be calibrated to the nature of the volunteer engagement. Of course, every institution has its own traditions which can used to make an award special.

The Yale Medal (*http://aya.yale.edu/content/yale-medal*). The Yale Medal is the highest award presented by the AYA, conferred solely to honor outstanding individual service to the University. In addition to the Medal itself, recipients' names are carved into the wood panels of Commons. Recipients do not necessarily have to be Yale degree holders, but most are. Each year, up to 5 recipients are chosen by a committee of the AYA Board of Governors. The Medal is given primarily and typically for volunteer service to Yale, so the committee rarely considers current or past members of the University administration, faculty or staff. The Medal is presented by the President of Yale during the annual AYA Assembly (joined in many years by those attending the Yale Alumni Fund Convocation) at a special dinner given at Commons in honor of the Yale Medal winners, and attended by approximately 500 volunteer leaders.

AYA Board of Governors Excellence Awards (*http://aya.yale.edu/content/aya-board-governors-excellence-awards*). These certificates recognize the superior accomplishments of Yale's classes, regional clubs and associations, shared identity and interest groups, and the graduate and professional school alumni associations. They recognize events, programs, and best practices. Recipients are chosen by a committee of the Board of Governors of the AYA, and written up for future reference: *https://docs.google.com/file/d/0B_xST13LJbZ_UXVpUmxTcTlYMUE/edit* . The Awards are presented by leadership of the AYA, during Assembly at a special awards reception.

AYA Leadership Awards for Volunteer Innovation and Service (*http://aya.yale.edu/content/aya-leadership-awards-volunteer-innovation-and-service*). This engraved pewter bowl is given to individual volunteers for extraordinary accomplishments, innovation and selfless service to AYA. The AYA staff chooses the recipients – 5 or 6 each year. The award is presented by leadership of the AYA, during Assembly at the awards reception. See link to *https://docs.google.com/file/d/0B_xST13LJbZ_UXVpUmxTcTlYMUE/edit* after pp. 48-51.

Class Awards (*http://aya.yale.edu/content/class-awards_2999*). AYA encourages Classes to bestow awards at their 5-year reunions to recognize and thank classmates who have dedicated time, energy and enthusiasm to the Class. Awardees are selected by the Class leadership.

Howard R. Lamar Faculty Award (*http://aya.yale.edu/content/howard-r-lamar-faculty-award*). The Howard R. Lamar Faculty Award is presented by the Board of Governors of the AYA, to a Yale faculty member to honor outstanding individual service to the alumni of Yale University, through a variety of alumni relations programs. Inaugurated in 2014, the first five recipients were chosen by a committee consisting of the Executive Committee of the Board of Governors including AYA professional staff. The Award was given in the spring.

Yale-Jefferson Public Service Awards (*http://aya.yale.edu/content/2014-award-winners-summaries*). Certificates are awarded to three Yalies — one alumnus, one graduate/professional student, and one undergraduate — who inspire others in the Yale community through innovative and sustained contributions of service to the greater good. They are given under the auspices of Students and Alumni for Yale (known as STAY, an AYA-supported student-alumni organization) and decided upon by a committee of student and University leaders. The awards are presented by a Yale Vice President at a Friday luncheon during AYA Assembly (joined in many years by those attending the Yale Alumni Fund Convocation) and attended by approximately 500 volunteer leaders.

7.3 | Leadership and Governance

Good governance is about the best processes for making and implementing decisions – but cannot guarantee "correct" decisions: *http://www.goodgovernance.org.au/about-good-governance/what-is-good-governance/*. According to this and many formulations, good governance is accountable, transparent, responsive, equitable and inclusive, effective and efficient, participatory, and follows the rule of law. But just saying so doesn't make it happen. Different organizations will require different rules to achieve this.

For some ways to ask the right questions about what rules and structures are best for an organization see *http://www.companydirectors.com.au/Director-Resource-Centre/Not-for-profit/Good-Governance-Principles-and-Guidance-for-NFP-Organisations* and *https://www.independentsector.org/uploads/PrincipleResources/The_33_Principles.pdf*.

Governance structures and roles engage volunteers. Well defined roles create entry points to the organization to engage volunteers. Roles need to be tailored to the different talents available. They need to be laddered so that volunteers can be engaged at their level of comfort – and so they can grow. Existing leadership and governance need to anticipate the needs of the organization and the talents of the upcoming leadership to make sure there is a match.

Governance structures and roles must fit the resources of the community that the organization serves. This is particularly true of voluntary associations and volunteer organizations. *The organization* *can only rely upon the time, talent, and treasure that its volunteers bring to the table.* For example, the rules can't require a larger quorum than usually come to a meeting. As another example, a top heavy volunteer organization with all leaders and few workers is likely to collapse. In contrast, a well-funded organization with professional paid managers and workers, may thrive with a large non-hands-on volunteer advisory board (whose primary responsibility may be giving or raising money). Sometimes an organization will be founded by a charismatic or superbly talented individual or group, but the intent of governance rules and structures is to enable the organization to continue to exist past the tenure of extraordinary founders – when roles must be filled by others in the community.

Rules of governance cultivate leadership. A documented set of rules (as you would have in a governing document such as by-laws) or job descriptions provide guidance for both expert and developing leaders and for different leadership roles. The rules may specify responsibilities, when things must be accomplished and what decisions must be made. They detail who is responsible for getting what done, and who must be consulted. When people are given leadership roles, the rules of governance help people grow into those roles. The rules, both formal and informal act like a handbook for leaders. However, it is still necessary for one generation of leaders to mentor the next. When you expect volunteers to do real work, and assume real responsibility, you must give them real power.

Rules of governance need to be tailored to the organization being governed. Certainly, many rules of governance may be dictated by law – which varies from country to country, and even province to province. Still it is important to consider the needs and purpose of the organization – both when setting up an organization, or reviewing its efficacy. This is true of all kinds of organizations, governments, for-profit enterprise, not-for-profit ones, and voluntary associations. This is true with respect to both formal written rules as well as informal and customary ones. The more a university expects its alumni organizations to be self-funded, and self-managed, the more control it has to give up.

Governance can help articulate community values, purpose, or vision, but cannot substitute for them. If an organization's (or a community's) leaders do not believe in these values, they will work around them. They may abide by the letter of the rules, without following their spirit. Besides, one cannot create a rule for every situation. In those cases, values must be internalized in the leaders. Building a community (or organization) and its values requires building a culture that embodies these values. It requires the patient and continued leadership of many individuals over time to instill a sense of community and community values in the group's members. And to create traditions that bind generations. These leaders must live these values, encouraging others by example.

Governance rules support leadership, volunteer recruitment, and good stewardship. The written or generally accepted rules and policies of the organization are a crucial support structure for the organization. However it is the implementation and the actions of the leadership that make an organization strong and successful.

Chapter 8

Organizing People

There are two distinct parts to organizing a group of people. One is motivating the individuals in the group to coalesce into a collectivity. The other is articulating a mission for that organization and creating a structure within which the collectivity's energies can be directed towards those goals. Having considered some of the governance or structural concepts in the previous chapter, this chapter will look at concepts of organizing people.

In brief, a group can be organized from the top down, or the bottom up. In either case, most volunteer-based organizations need to be organized around a shared passion. Sometimes the organizer's task is recognizing the group to be organized. Sometimes it is recognizing the passion.

8.1 | Affinity Groups
organizing alumni affinity groups

An Affinity Group is a set of people who share a common interest or identity.

Affinity groups have been organizing for centuries as dining clubs, fraternal organizations, guilds, athletic associations, political action groups, and social change collectivities. Alumni affinity groups at university have been organizing at least since the 1850s, when Yale alumni self-organized to form the "Crew Association" to support undergraduate rowing at Yale. More recently, especially since the turn of the twenty-first century, university alumni relations departments and associations have found affinity groups based on identity or other shared interests to be an effective way to engage alumni across classes, regions and schools, as well as within classes, regions and schools.

Affinity groups can be organized from the top down or from the bottom up. In other words, the university may be instrumental in promoting the formation of specific alumni affinity groups that are of institutional interest, or the university can provide a climate and culture in its alumni relations that enables self-organization among the alumni in such groups. Generally, there is an element of both.

Organizing alumni affinity groups originating at the university. A recent example is the formation of YaleWomen as a world-wide affinity group within AYA. The process involved both the AYA and Yale – and active Yale alumnae leaders. Both AYA and Yale invested considerable resources to encourage and nurture the formation of the group. For a Case Study, see *www.yalegale.org/resources/wp-content/uploads/2013/01/YaleWomen-Case-Study-011413.pdf* . The institution can increase the chances of success by some crucial early steps:

- ❑ **Hold one or more galvanizing events** of interest to potential members and leaders of the group. Use the gatherings as a way to build a database of potential members and leaders. If more than one event, engage some of those enthused by the first event to help plan the second. Use to recruit leaders for the next step.

- ❑ **Help stage a strategic planning retreat.** Make sure that significant aspects of the planning come from leaders emerging from the earlier events. Provide expert consultants and facilitators so that the new organization develops a community and a plan.

- ❑ **Provide ongoing database, communications, and organizational support.**

The aims of community organizing for social action are different than a university's alumni engagement so the standard guidelines about tactics and specific plans for social action often differ from those of a university. Nonetheless some of the insights are still crucial. For example, to become involved people must see (a) a benefit to themselves or others that they want to assist if the group succeeds (or risk to themselves if the group fails) and (b) their involvement will make a difference. For other important teachings, including that the most important victory is the group itself, see: *http://comm-org.wisc.edu/papers97/beckwith.htm* . See also *http://www.worc.org/media/Howto-Understand-Role-of-Community-Organizer.pdf* .

Organizing alumni affinity groups from the bottom up. A recent example is the explosive growth of Yale in Hollywood. The original idea for an entertainment industry affinity group came from a subgroup of the Yale Club of Southern California. The organizers of one event found the attendees so enthused and eager for more, that they proceeded to organize larger events and are now bi-coastal. Some local chapters of YaleWomen were organized from the bottom up. See *www.yalegale.org/resources/wp-content/uploads/2014/07/YaleWomen_starting_chapters.pdf*. One formulation details five simple action items (*http://localcircles.org/2012/05/17/what-is-an-affinity-group/*):

❑ Start with a handful of people you know.

❑ Do something soon.

❑ Learn consensus building and how small groups can make decisions effectively.

❑ Bring all of yourself - build friends and community, not just an action group.

❑ Meet over a meal.

An alternate formulation of organizing tips from *http://www.occupylv.org/spokes-council-organizing-affinity-groups* is "Form a group with your friends! Be loud! Look exciting! Have fun!"

8.2 | Organizing Alumni by Interests and Passions

Which comes first— a group with a shared passion that becomes organized into a formal entity or a passion that is so compelling that many people choose to organize around it?

You can organize a Shared Interest Group (SIG) or Affinity Group by first identifying a group to be organized. That group can be organized from the top down, the bottom up, or some combination (see above).

Alternatively you can identify an interest or passion (for an activity) to organize around. Often this distinction will not matter. But, starting with a shared interest in doing an activity may lend a different dynamic to the collectivity.

In some alumni-based SIGs, this different dynamic is caused by focusing on organizing an annual (or periodic) participatory event or activity rather than (a) organizing a group to support current students who are engaged in that activity or (b) organizing a group for intergroup networking opportunities. Sometimes, the organizational motivation is *for alumni to do now what they had loved to do as students* – with a group of like-minded individuals.

Some examples of organizing around a passion once held as students:

Yale Alumni Chorus. The Yale Alumni Chorus (YAC) is a self-funded member-based organization. It produces choral concert tours and participates in festivals. Hundreds of alumni, family and friends participate in each program. Many view this as a proto-typical SIG, but it did not arise as an alumni continuation of a specific student group. Certainly Yale has a long tradition of multiple undergraduate (and graduate student) singing groups that go on tour. Many of these choral groups have their own alumni SIGs which provide support and guidance. In contrast, YAC was founded by alumni who just wanted to sing together as Yalies (*http://alumninet.yale.edu/sigs/yac/aboutus.html*).

AYA Service Initiatives. Since 2008, the Association of Yale Alumni has developed several alumni-run service initiatives: Yale Alumni Service Corps (*yaleservicecorps.org*), Yale Global Alumni Leadership Exchange (*yalegale.org*), and Yale Day of Service (*yaledayofservice.org*). Each has different programs and organizational characteristics.

❏ **Yale Alumni Service Corps:** Every year, hundreds of Yale alumni, family and friends travel to a developing country, or an under-developed community to perform community service. Projects range from education to public health to light construction. Each trip is self-funded by the alumni who participate in it.

❏ **Yale Global Alumni Leadership Exchange:** Every year, a delegation of Yale alumni, family and friends travel abroad at their own expense to exchange best practices in alumni relations with foreign universities.

❏ **Yale Day of Service:** On the Yale Day of Service (DoS), alumni and their families and friends work side by side to make communities better because Yale alumni live there. The effort involves over 4000 Yale alumni, family and friends at over 250 sites around the world. Many DoS projects are part of ongoing efforts by local Yale Clubs or other Yale alumni organizations – and part of their programming toolkit.

Yale has a long history of student-run community service and social justice initiatives. While the AYA service initiatives are not affiliated with any of the specific Yale student service programs, they tap into a passion of many alumni for performing service to their community (or communities around the world) under the banner of Yale.

Dernell Every Fencing Tournament. This tournament is a yearly fundraising event organized by the Yale Fencing Association – an alumni SIG which supports the Yale Fencing Team. The unique feature of this tournament is that Yale alums who had been on the Fencing Team as students compete against current Yale student fencers. It gives current fencers and alums a chance to get together for a friendly day of fencing and camaraderie – to bond the way a sports team does, via competition. (*http://www.yalebulldogs.com/sports/m-fenc/2009-10/releases/20091119xaocy1*).

Feb Club Emeritus. Feb Club was originally an undergraduate student social event. However, since 2008, it has become a social event for alumni around the world *(www.febclub.webs.com)*. The student tradition was an attempt to enliven the coldest, dampest month of the year – February – by holding a party at Yale every night of the month. As an alumni tradition the intent is to hold an alumni get-together (no matter how small) somewhere in the world every night of February. Many Yale regional associations participate, sometimes sponsoring several events to serve a dispersed constituency. There are currently over 100 Feb Club events around the globe attended by over 5000 alumni.

8.3 | Creating a Community around Travel

The alumni connection can be a powerful motivator – and innovator – of international opportunities. It's especially true in the context of a world where travel is expected for a well-educated person and collaborative efforts take place half-way around the globe. Beginning about 50 years ago, a few universities began to offer trips that fit the educational mission of the university while generating some additional support for other alumni relation efforts. Today opportunities for alumni engagement and travel have expanded to a range of new programs that encourage alumni to follow their passions by traveling with others who share an interest – or an affinity – for a particular activity. The affinity travel experience can create a community for those who share the overlapping interests. Or, an affinity based community can choose to travel and form tighter bonds for having shared an intense experience.

Yale Educational Travel (*www.yaleedtravel.org*), part of the Association of Yale Alumni, offers a range of affinity or educational travel that includes adventure tours, family tours, photography tours, theater tours, and various cruises. Smaller alumni groups also do this. Recently, the Yale Club of Washington, organized a successful lecture tour of the Civil War Battlefield at Gettysburg to generate funds for the Club: *www.yaleedtravel.org/programs/10153* .

It is more than the destination, the theme, or the purpose – it's the package. Packaging the journey is necessary to create community, but not sufficient. Compare *http://en.wikipedia.org/wiki/Package_tour* .

A key piece of a successful tour package is the social interaction. The consumer who buys a package gives up flexibility and customization for **convenience, value** (perhaps cost savings or special access), assured **quality and responsibility – and perhaps primarily for social interaction.** Consumers seek others with sufficient affinities to have good dinner and touring conversations during the trip. This is why affinity travel is so successful.

Community requires continuity, and ownership. To be a community of travelers – especially a community of volunteers traveling together – rather than just participants in a trip, a significant number of the travelers must feel ownership of the journey and will often become the most frequent participants. The strongest community is created when some of the travelers are also volunteers as they help plan, organize, and administer the travel. Community members may have different roles: tourist, traveler, guide, or leader – a community requires all four. Here is the concept adapted from "The 3 Stages of the Volunteer": *www.realizedworth.com/2012/05/3-stages-of-volunteer-what-they-need.html* which uses these terms metaphorically rather than literally as done here:

❑ **Tourist.** They are first here to enjoy the ride, and can be given specific tasks, and shown how to do them. A majority of participants in the travel activity may be tourists ready to appreciate the sense of community and, perhaps, become more engaged. Use the techniques of volunteer engagement including support and thanks. (See Chapter 6.)

❑ **Traveler.** They know what to do, but need permission to do it. They may be ready to take on responsibility, but will do it their own way. Don't burn them out or give them tasks beyond them. As your potential future leaders it is worth investing extra effort to manage them. Use the techniques of cultivating leadership. (See Chapter 7.) Follow up and nurture their interest.

❑ **Guide.** These leaders can be trusted to run parts or all of the program thanks to their talent and experience. Follow up and thank them!

❑ **Leader.** They are ready to take the lead in designing a new program either within the existing framework or a variation or new concept. The organization needs creative people like this – and they need the support of all the other participants. Follow up and thank them most of all – both to convey your appreciation and to inspire others to lead.

Travel communities can be organized from the top down or the bottom up.
- ❏ **Yale Alumni Chorus** (*http://alumninet.yale.edu/sigs/yac/aboutus.html*) was organized by volunteers from the bottom up. They wanted to sing with other Yalies and give concerts around the world.
- ❏ **Yale Alumni Service Corps** (*www.yaleservicecorps.org*) was initially organized by AYA from the top down, but has since become a self-governing community engaged in providing service in underserved communities around the world.

Successful affinity-based travel can form the basis of a community. Whether performance-based (e.g. singing), sports-based (e.g. skiing, golfing, biking), service-based, adventure-based (e.g. bird watching) or otherwise – if the alumni collectivity (or market) is large enough, a community can be built by giving them ownership. For more on affinity and shared interest groups see Chapter 3.4 and Chapter 8.

8.4 | Building Alumni Community through Athletics

Traditional sport rivalries between universities can re-engage all alumni on an annual basis. *However, among those alumni who were student athletes, a tighter knit alumni community can be developed.*

Student athletes are fiercely passionate about their sport. They expend intense amounts of time and energy with team members and coaches. They work tirelessly and fearlessly to excel in competition. Spending so much time together in pursuit of common goals builds strong friendships with teammates – and a student's identity with a particular sport runs deep. When the team is part of the university, a student's loyalty to the team can translate into loyalty to the university. This loyalty to team, teammates and sponsoring university can continue as students become alumni and can continue for a lifetime.

Alumni athletic associations can nurture loyalty to fellow team members and the university. For example, at Yale, self-organized alumni athletic associations were the first shared interest groups

(SIGs). Alumni used them to provide monetary support for equipment and coaches to current student teams as well as networking and career support for alumni who had been team members. This sense of ongoing family may translate into more general support for the University. See Athletics overview in 3.4.1.

Friendly competition among athletic team alumni can strengthen friendships and develop new ones. It can continue to build on the emotional bonds that developed among teammates who competed together. It can help develop new bonds among athletes of different generations. Possibilities among non-contact sports are myriad. They can build sustainable traditions that support team and university. For example,

❑ Yale's swimming and diving teams have a Blue Legends Alumni Swim during their annual winter alumni weekend.

❑ The Yale golf team annually has an alumni golf outing in the fall.

❑ Yale's men's and women's crew (rowing) teams regularly host alumni rows during reunions, large events, or just because a few former teammates called their head coach to request it. In conjunction with endowing their head coach position, the women's team recently celebrated their 40th anniversary with six teams of alumni "eights" racing!

Such competition is facilitated in many sports through recognized systems of age handicapping. Others have traditions (often called "pro-am" for professional-amateur) of pairing more robust or skilled players with less skilled ones. Still others, such as basketball, reduce contact aspects of the sport for older athletes.

Athletes like to engage through sport – even new sports. Golf is a favorite and can be the basis of friendly but competitive outings among former teammates. For example, Yale's golf course hosts an annual alumni event for the volleyball, soccer, hockey, football, basketball and lacrosse alumni associations.

Friendly competition between alumni and students can build important networks. The potential advantage of such competitions is that it creates friendships and networks that bridge generations, and can result in connections that help students get jobs when they graduate. Former athletes understand the teamwork and focus that young athletes can bring to any job. These intergenerational networks strengthen the sense of family among team alumni – and a sense that the university is part of that family. In some sports athletes remain competitive for many years and can compete directly with younger ones, especially when honed skill, hand-eye coordination, or the elements of teamwork are more central than raw force or speed. Consider fencing, archery, or sailing. For example:

❑ The Yale Association holds the Dernell Every Tournament as an annual event when alumni can fence against current student fencers, followed by a banquet.

❑ The Yale Sailing Team has an annual spring alumni regatta which current students often join.

See also 11.4 Planning Multiple-Location Events using social media, for other ways to organize people.

Chapter 9

Creating Organizations

A group may have passion, but viable organization of the group won't just happen. Formal aspects of creating an organization involve building a structure that will conserve and channel the group's passion. Tasks include strategic planning, mission discernment, and governance documents. This chapter focuses on these issues. Much of this may be volunteer driven, but tasks like strategic planning, mission discernment, or drafting governance documents may require involving an expert or facilitator.

For additional information see two online case studies of YaleWomen, an affinity group for Yale alumna. The one case study narrates how YaleWomen was organized as a (national) group: *www.yalegale.org/resources/wp-content/uploads/2013/01/YaleWomen-Case-Study-011413.pdf* . The second details the subsequent creation of YaleWomen regional chapters: *www.yalegale.org/resources/wp-content/uploads/2014/07/YaleWomen_starting_chapters.pdf* .

9.1 | Strategic Planning for an alumni relations organization

The typical components of a strategic plan are relevant for alumni relations organizations, including mission, vision, values, goals, strategies, tactics, and outcomes metrics, along with associated action and financial plans. This holds true with respect to both the umbrella organization and its constituent organizations such as regional associations, classes and affinity groups.

Yet in some ways strategic planning for an alumni organization is different from other contexts. Not all official stakeholders may have an active interest in the organization. For example, not all the alumni who are part of a group (by definition) may identify with the group or its objectives – and some may not choose to be engaged with that specific group. The strategic planning process can be used to both identify what the strategic priorities and desired outcomes are, and serve as a method to create stronger alumni connections and build a volunteer cohort that will help execute and advocate for the plan. A good strategic planning process can identify alumni that had not formerly been involved and motivate them to get involved. Alumni organizations can also use the strategic plan to identify their resource requirements and budget needs.

There are some unique issues which alumni relations organizations may need to consider during a strategic planning process, such as:

Structure

❑ What is the formal governance relationship between the university and the alumni association?

❑ What is the alumni organization's financial and business model (e.g., membership paid or not?)

❑ What is the relationship between alumni relations and development? Are these activities housed within a single alumni relations organization, or are they separated into two distinct organizations that work cooperatively?

❑ What are the current volunteer structures (roles/ responsibilities) and how might they change because of the plan?

Process

❑ What are the objectives of the plan, in the context of the mission and structure of the alumni organization?

❑ What is the input and decision making process to create and approve the plan?

❑ How can the alumni association engage a broad range of alumni by age, geographic location, and interests?

❑ What communications messages and vehicles are needed to inform and engage the full alumni population once the plan is completed?

Content

❑ What is the scope of issues the strategic plan needs to address, from engagement to giving?

❑ How does the alumni association's mission promote the range of ways alumni engage with the university, and does the structure of the organization enable that?

❑ How can alumni, through the alumni relations organization, advance university's "institutional" priories?

The principle stakeholders in an alumni relations strategic plan can include the alumni relations and development volunteer leadership, the broader alumni population, university leadership, and alumni relations and development staff.

Recommendations. Use the strategic planning process as a way to engage alumni and make sure they become advocates for the plan. Ask alumni directly how the organization can better meet their needs and the needs of the university. To do this, you need to go where the alumni already are, what would be called the natural connection points. Alumni engagement should take place intensively during the planning process to help shape the plan and once the plan is complete, key directions should be shared broadly with alumni and to reconnect with (potential) alumni leaders.

Sample strategic plans

❑ Association of Yale Alumni – Yale Ambassadors in Action, 2012: http://www.aya.yale.edu/sites/default/files/images/AYA%20Strategic%20Plan%202%200 0%20-%20FINAL%20-%20 for%20web.pdf

❑ Association of Yale Alumni – Ambassadors for Yale, 2008: http://www.aya.yale.edu/sites/default/files/docs/AYA_StrategicPlan2008.pdf

❏ YaleWomen – A New Alumnae Network, 2011: *http://d3n8a8pro7vhmx.cloudfront.net/yalewomen/pages/1/attachments/original/1374779194/Yale_Women_Strategic_Plan_Dec_2011.pdf?1374779194*

9.2 | Advanced Strategic Planning through bold ideas

Ideation *(the formation of ideas or concepts)* **is foundational to the development of a strategic plan.** It is essential in order to move the alumni relations effort forward in a bold way. At the same time, effective strategy calls for a meaningful assessment of the attractiveness and feasibility of each idea among those generated. Clear priorities among an often wide ranging set of ideas need to be established.

In the early stages of the strategic planning process, tap peer groups and engage diverse stakeholder groups to identify a broad range of ideas. Ask what your alumni relations organization could do or be. Such outreach ensures a rich context for strategic planning discussions.

Why Bold Ideas are Important

Without bold ideas, an organization can get into a rut. Without innovative approaches, it will be destined to implement the same tactics in the same ways. As its audience evolves, the organization may attract and serve a smaller and smaller portion of them. Bold ideas are required to enlarge and engage a changing constituency.

Examples of Bold Ideas in Alumni Relations at Yale

- ❏ Organizing around Shared Interest Groups instead of just classes and geographic clubs
- ❏ YaleWomen
- ❏ Yale Veterans Association (alumni who have served in the military)
- ❏ Supporting alumni self-organizing (a fundamental governance decision)

- Feb Club (Yalies self-organize to party around the world)
- Yale alumni Civil War trip (educational travel organized by volunteers of a regional association to generate operational funds for the association)
- Providing opportunities for Yalies to serve the broader community under the auspices of the alumni organization and with other Yalies
- Yale Day of Service (once a year, Yalies will be called upon to provide local community service together)
- YaleGALE (volunteers sharing best practices in alumni relations with other people and institutions from around the world)
- Enhancing alumni-student interactions and programming opportunities

Some other possible Bold Ideas
- Developing innovative metrics and methodologies to measure program success
- Exploring innovative ways to fund programs

Characteristics of Bold Ideas

Bold ideas challenge assumptions in new and interesting ways. In essence, they are sometimes unsettling. The bolder the idea, the more change is involved – and therefore the greater likelihood for both current stakeholders and/or current leadership to reject the idea ("That's not how we do things here" or "We tried something like that and it failed"). Bold ideas might be generated by potential new leadership. Consider taking advantages of new opportunities caused by disintermediation. Examine where new technologies and social media platforms provide blank canvases for re-imagining existing activities. For example, how can Facebook and social media make in-person reunions bigger and better? Or, how does social media create opportunities for new forms of alumni engagement, including self-organizing?

Idea Generation and Implementation during the Life of a Strategic Plan

Creating and implementing a strategic plan is a multi-step process intended to discern the mission of the organization and address the needs of the identifiable constituencies over time. The life of a strategic plan includes both the time for generating the plan and the time for executing it. While the strategic planning process may typically take at least 6 months to generate the plan, it will then take up to 5 years to carry out the plan (with benchmarking and reassessment opportunities along the way).

In the context of Bold Ideas, the process can be broken into the following steps:

Idea generation

- ❑ **Inventory.** What ideas are already in the system?

- ❑ **Assumptions.** What does the group see as necessary or needed – and what can be changed? Think carefully about the opportunities for stopping current practices that may no longer be relevant.

- ❑ **Peers.** What do other institutions do? Ask people around campus for ideas.

- ❑ **Alumni.** What do alumni think? Make sure to engage alumni early in the process and get ideas from as many people as possible, not just leaders who may like the current programs. Try to get ideas that would engage alumni who have not been involved.

Filtering the big list

- ❑ **Impact.** Which ideas will have the most impact in achieving the mission of the alumni association? Of the university? Of the alumni? If the strategic planning process generates a "new" mission or "new" metrics, gauge impact in terms of this new thinking.

- ❑ **Resources.** Which ideas are practical based on the professional team, the departmental budget, and volunteer leadership?

- ❑ **Commitment.** Who will lead the change? For each bold idea, make sure that you know there will be a committed leader for the program. This will most likely be a volunteer and most likely the person (or people) who proposed it.

Idea to execution

- ❑ **Planning.** How will the idea be fleshed out? Every bold idea needs its own planning process that focuses on purpose and logistics. Strong leadership and institutional support are essential.
- ❑ **Ownership.** Who will follow through? You always need a leader – or two! Who "owns" the idea among the professional team and who owns it among the volunteers?
- ❑ **Piloting.** How will the idea be tested? The bolder the idea, the more important it is to have a test or pilot phase for proof of concept. Make sure that it serves the mission. Make sure it is manageable. Piloting an idea allows flexibility and manages expectations of participants (and the administration). Piloting paves the way for a bigger subsequent commitment.
- ❑ **Life cycle.** What is the idea's life expectancy? When adopting a bold idea, consider the expected life cycle of the project. Consider not only the length of time to plan it, but also the number of years that it might exist, as well as the opportunities to measure its success and re-design it. Some programs might unfold quarterly and get reassessed once a year while others might be annual events that need to be reconsidered each time.

Ongoing idea sourcing

- ❑ **Engagement.** How will engagement foster new ideas? As the strategic planning and the implementation of ideas happens over the years, include processes to continue to identify new ideas. Often new leaders that engage in a program come up with new ideas that had not occurred to them during the planning process.
- ❑ **Assessment.** What are the metrics? When deciding to pursue a new idea, decide on the expected and desired outcome in advance. In other words, think about the metrics and what is measurable as part of the planning process so you can assess your success along the way. The assessment process can also lead to new ideas.

❏ **Adaptability.** How can the idea evolve? Many of the best ideas come from adapting a bold idea from its initial pilot incarnation into something that is more effective – or even from an old idea that has been re-designed. Remember, even the best programs have to adapt over time in consideration of changing interests and new technology.

A successful strategic planning process will intentionally seek out and explore a range of ideas. A plan that propels the alumni organization forward will likely need a combination of ideas that are bold (giant steps) and others that are more incremental in nature (baby steps). Cast a wide net. Then rigorously filter the big list of ideas. This creates a platform for a strategic plan with impact and enhanced alumni engagement.

See also 7.3 Leadership and Governance

Chapter 10

Developing a Culture and Shared Values

Getting alumni to come back to campus, to want to get together with other alumni, and ultimately to give back, requires creating a community and a sense of connectedness. This is also an important ingredient in getting volunteers to continue being involved in a particular organization – because after all, there are usually a number of organizations that share the same passion. Part of this is nurturing a set of values linked to the organization. Part of this is creating shared (and enjoyable) experiences linked to the organization. Part is creating a shared sense of place and tradition.

10.1 | Building a Culture of connection and loyalty

Infusing and nurturing loyalty and connectedness starts before students become alumni. It starts when they are first admitted as students – sometimes even before that. It continues for a lifetime.

The university's opportunity. Universities have a unique opportunity to create a bond with their students, because the experiences and adventures of one's youth are those that most people remember most intensely. Particularly poignant are the memories of "growing up", transitioning from child to adult, being "on one's own" for the first time. For many these start in the late teenage years and continue through undergraduate (or graduate) years at university.

The university's challenge. As the mission of every university is centered on education and research, the challenge is to create an environment that also builds community and loyalty among the students as well as the faculty and administration. Students may have to work hard for their education and are constantly being graded so their memories and associations with the university may not be all positive. Nonetheless, universities need to work to give students fond memories that bind them to the university rather than just ones which are distancing or distasteful. The idea is to make both students and alumni feel like family.

The admissions process. The community building process starts when a potential student first visits a university or when he or she is first interviewed as part of an admissions process as at many U.S. institutions. The applicant, just like students, needs to be treated with the respect and concern one would accord a potential family member – not just a customer. The university has to inculcate a sense of appreciation and responsibility to future generations while they educate the students regardless of whether funding is from the government or from donors or from tuition. A university education cannot seem like just a commodity or an entitlement, it needs to be a unique and valuable community experience.

A community of students. What binds alumni most strongly to each other and for a lifetime are the connections and friendships that they made as students. This is more than just sitting in a classroom together. The social glue comes from the extra-curricular life: studying together, working together on projects or campus jobs, competing together on athletic teams, eating together, playing together, singing together, living in close proximity, and socializing together.

Young people will have these interactions whether or not the university orchestrates or facilitates them. However, if the university sponsors those activities, and designs them with care, alumni will believe that the strongest friendships in their lives were due in part to the environment and good graces of the university. They will view the university fondly and as a true alma mater. In contrast, if they believe the best part of their youth occurred despite university discouragement, they are not likely to feel moved to give back to university.

Student activities. Student activities introduce students to future spouses, companions, and business partners. Student activities teach important leadership and workplace skills not taught in the classroom: how to manage one's time, how to work in a team, and how to manage others. At Yale University approximately 500 student activities serve its 5400 undergraduates: *http://yaledailynews.com/blog/2014/04/09/up-close-how-many-is-too-many/*. They include sports teams (varsity, club, and intramural), singing groups (large choruses and a cappella), debating societies, political forums across the spectrum, film groups (both watching and creating), print media (newspapers, literary magazines, and humor periodicals), service and social justice organizations, dance groups (ethnic and contemporary), performance groups (dramatic, comedic, and improvisational), identity groups (religious, ethnic, lifestyle, and sexual orientation), symphonies (plus chamber groups and a marching band), eating clubs, a literary society, fraternities, sororities, and much more: *http://en.wikipedia.org/wiki/List_of_Yale_University_student_organizations*. The effectiveness of these activities in building loyalty is confirmed by all the alumni shared interest groups they have spawned. See Chapter 3.4.

Mentoring. For some students, similar connections extend to the faculty and coaches who taught them. This may be especially true for students who themselves become academics, or students whose research internships or team experiences became the basis for their post-university careers. But it also holds when students have gained insight from a strong mentoring relationship with a faculty member. Some alumni fondly remember university and professorial interactions as the one time in their life when a thirst for learning could be expressed without reservation. The university can encourage such student-professor interactions. Yale demonstrates that they are not incompatible with a research university.

A network of alumni. Intergenerational networking (and intra-generational networking) can be key elements in a successful career. University alumni organizations can be instrumental in building these networks. But they are also built when a student's professor (or former professor) helps make a contact or assists in obtaining an internship for a student.

Architecture and campus design. Architecture can both enhance those memories and provide a setting which facilitates them. Not only is beautiful architecture memorable, but the design of university spaces can enable and assist the social interactions which bind people to each other in the context of a place. See Chapter 10.3 on the Architecture of Return and the Campus as a Curated Gallery of fine architecture.

10.2 | Parents as donors and community members

Universities have to balance their outreach to parents. *On the one hand, they want parents to feel welcome,* and to be members of the university community, so they willingly pay tuition, so that they spread good will for the university in their own communities, and so that they feel comfortable talking to the university about their children if difficulties occur. Universities want to engage parents so that they support university activities (sports teams, cultural activities, educational initiatives), both politically and economically – as spectators, attendees, voters, advocates, consumers, donors and sometimes volunteers. When parents are enthusiastic and loyal supporters of a university, it can go a long way towards modeling that behavior in their children, the future alumni. *At the same time, universities do not want to be too welcoming,* because they do not want the parents visiting too often, interfering with students' lives as they grow up. And once students graduate, the university wants there to be a difference between an alumnus/a, and a non-alumni parent of a former student.

Fundraising and the Parents Fund. The development offices of many universities actively seek donations from parents of current and former students. Examples include the Yale University Parents Fund (*http://www.giftguide.yale.edu/opportunity/show/648*) and the Harvard University Parents Fund (*http://alumni.harvard.edu/college/college-giving/parents*). In some universities, parents may become a member of a special committee or parents' advisory board with its own networking events or advisory role. Sometimes this may be tied to a leadership gift from the parents.

Parent oriented activities. Many universities in the U.S. have special activities for parents several times during the year. These may include participation in "preview weekend" when accepted students visit the university, orientation weekend when parents accompany their child to start university, or on a designated family weekend in the fall semester.

Universities may nominally declare parents to be part of a Parents Association without dues. These non-fundraising activities are designed to bolster parent support, foster parent-child-family support, and ease transition of high school students into the university community. Universities keep in touch with parents while their children are students, through special newsletters or copies of the alumni magazine. Parents are invited to attend events when on campus. Parents who are celebrated in their field of endeavor may be asked to give talks or presentations about it.

Active Parent Associations. Some universities have Parent Associations which provide opportunities for parents to help with preview weekend, orientation weekend or family weekend, and at other times during the year. The extent of the volunteering, networking opportunities and independence of the Parent Association varies. Parent Association volunteers may be involved with outreach, such as contacting parents of newly admitted students to answer questions, or hosting receptions in their home town for new students about to attend the university. Links to some specific university volunteer opportunities.

❑ Stanford Parents Club: *http://web.stanford.edu/group/parentsclub/*

❑ MIT Parents Association: *http://parents.mit.edu/* and their "Parent Connectors" *http://parents.mit.edu/s/1314/04-parents/index.aspx?sid=1314&gid=31&pgid=1117*

❑ Johns Hopkins University: *http://parents.jhu.edu/volunteer/index.html* (volunteering opportunities) and *http://parents.jhu.edu/pin/index.html* (Parents Internship Network, parents offering internships for students)

❑ Vanderbilt University: *http://www.vanderbilt.edu/families/association/*

❑ George Washington University in Wash., D.C.: *http://parents.gwu.edu/get-involved*

Dues. Some Parent Associations have membership fees or dues, with benefits such as discounts on merchandise with the university logo or better access to tickets to university sporting events. (See Texas Parents, of the University of Texas, Austin: *http://www.texasparents.org/ membership_fouryears.php*.)

Interface with the University Alumni Association. Some universities invite parents to regional association events, including family events. Others allow parents to join their alumni association while the child is at university. The University of Michigan has such a membership turn into a lifetime membership for the child when the child graduates: *http://alumni.umich.edu/join-the-alumni-association/ parent* . At least one university (University of Michigan) has a family camp in which parents and children can participate together. Camp Michigania is exclusive for members of the alumni association, but including parent non-alumni members: *http://alumni.umich.edu/ connect/michigania* .

10.3 | The Architecture of Return

Does distinctive Campus architecture matter to students who do not study architecture? *Is there a function or purpose to university buildings besides educating students and supporting faculty (or pleasing donors)?*

Certainly the primary function of a university is educating students and supporting faculty research. However, in today's world, the importance of alumni relations is increasing. This is because the long term health of the institution is enhanced when alumni continue to support the institution, such as by

❑ hiring and mentoring younger alumni

❑ recommending the institution to prospective students

❑ raising the profile of the institution by crediting some of their success to it

❑ donating funds to the institution

This happens when alumni remember their university fondly and with pride. This happens when alumni think of the university as their alma mater and fellow alumni as part of their family. Consequently, a campus architecture that creates a sense of family, nurtures memories of that place and those familial bonds, can contribute to the growth and sustenance of the university.

Yale has a wealth of beautiful buildings, a veritable sculpture garden of the works of some of the world's greatest architects. It also has nurturing residential facilities (called residential colleges), either originally designed or subsequently renovated to promote collegiality and interaction among students. Each has a Common Room, Dining Hall, and courtyard, with rooms for exercise, avocations, studying and just hanging out. Each has its own intramural athletic teams, and informal student run eateries. Each has a mix of living units, primarily focused on student suites built on an entryway system, rather than on corridors.

"The residential college system is one of the glories of Yale, and it is a major reason why students choose to come to Yale and a major reason why Yale College students report greater satisfaction with their education than students at most peer institutions," *http://newresidentialcolleges.yale.edu/vision/charting-course-academics-and-student-life#parameters* .

What draws alumni back to Campus for reunions, are not just memories of the place – but of memories of people. These significant social interactions are generated by the residential college design. The Yale Campus impacts its students directly if sometimes subconsciously. They remember those places. They want to come back to them.

To get a sense of this, read some of the online Architectural Remembrances prepared for YaleGALE – recollections of Yale alumni about spaces and places at Yale. Some concern specific pieces of architecture, some concern the spaces between them, some the friendship engendered thereby. See: *www.yalegale.org/resources/wp-content/uploads/2014/12/Architectural_remembrances_condensed.pdf* .

10.3.1 | The Campus as a Curated Gallery of fine architecture

Is a Campus just a group of buildings? *Can an architectural "collection" serve an educational purpose?*

This depends upon what a school wants to teach its students — and how it wants to teach it to them. But consider how Robert A.M. Stern revitalized the Yale School of Architecture in his time as Dean starting in 1998.

As an architect, he has won prizes and accolades. Many architectural critics believe that, under his leadership, the Yale School of Architecture returned from blandness to become one of the best and most exciting architecture schools in the world. Many critics and commentators feel this way despite the fact that they dislike the buildings that Robert Stern (the architect as opposed to the educator) designs. Rather, they appreciate what he has done for the School and the students taught there: *http://archpaper.com/news/articles.asp?id=3007* .

Dean Stern is praised for bringing a diversity of stellar architects, with an extraordinary range of styles, to teach at Yale. These include architects such as Frank Gehry, Zaha Hadid, Greg Lynn, David Adjaye, and Peter Eisenman. He has exposed the architecture students to these extra-ordinary yet differing architects. Some have even said that Dean Stern has "curated" a faculty of star architects.

Yet a famous architect who visits a university can interact with only some students and for a limited time. Most importantly, whether an architect is on campus teaching or not, many students on many campuses can experience that architect's buildings, if one of the architect's buildings is nearby.

The Curated Campus: Consider the Yale University Campus, in New Haven, Connecticut. The central parts of campus, including the residential dormitories, are primarily neoclassical. Many are red-brick Georgian and grey-stone Collegiate Gothic. Much of that was designed by the celebrated James Gamble Rogers. But there is also Greek-revivalist among them. Buildings constructed since the 1950s take a different approach.

Interspersed are magnificent and striking modern buildings by Louis I. Kahn, Paul Rudolph, Cesar Pelli, Eero Saarinen, Gordon Bunshaft, Robert Venturi, Philip Johnson, Frank Gehry, along with others.

For a map of many of these buildings, see *http://visitorcenter.yale.edu/sites/default/files/files/archtour_map.pdf* .

For photos and descriptions of a select number of these buildings, see *http://www.yale.edu/architectureofyale/*.

This curation of excellent architecture is an ongoing process, as new buildings are erected (see for example Kroon Hall, *https://environment. yale.edu/kroon/*, or Evans Hall, *http://www.architectmagazine.com/ design/buildings/edward-p-evans-hall-designed-by-foster-partners_o*) and other buildings are lovingly restored and renovated (see for example *http://www.nytimes.com/2008/08/28/arts/design/28yale. html*).

Yale is not alone in this planning scheme. Consider the campus of the California Institute of Technology (CalTech) in Pasadena, California. There are some striking similarities about the layout, planning, and design of CalTech's campus and Yale's – despite their many differences, including their educational focus.

- ❏ CalTech is a much smaller university than Yale. (12,000 students at Yale, 2,000 at CalTech)
- ❏ CalTech has a much smaller campus. (837 acres at Yale, 124 acres at CalTach)
- ❏ California's regional architecture is Spanish colonial. Yale's is New England colonial.
- ❏ California's semi-tropical vegetation is quite different than temperate Connecticut's.

However, both use courtyard-based residential facilities as an interesting but neutral palette from which spring surprising, delightful and carefully chosen modern buildings. This is much the way paintings are acquired and hung in a gallery space, or on a museum wall. See: *http://cats.caltech.edu/tourdesc* . Such a "curated" method for planning a growing campus may not suit all, but is certainly worth considering.

10.4 | Building Community through symbol, ritual and tradition

One role of any alumni organization is to create, nurture, transform, support and enhance rituals and traditions that can serve to strengthen its community.

Symbols, rituals, and traditions create a university's brand. They distinguish one university from another. But rituals and traditions do much more when they are participatory experiences, or reminders of those experiences.

- ❑ They create strong memories which bind alumni to the time and place of their youth at university.

- ❑ They create common memories among graduates who attended university together, but did not know each other there, or did not have other common interests.

- ❑ They create a similar experience and a sense of shared memories for multiple generations of students and people from different eras.

- ❑ They can also reflect cultural values that reflect the institution's values and bind generations together.

- ❑ They can sometimes offer alumni not just memories, but a way to continue to participate in traditions, along with other alumni and students, and re-experience their transformative effects.

In his works, Randall Collins discusses how social interactions and rituals bind groups together. (For a quick look at what his work suggests for alumni relations, see *http://alumnivolunteer.org/binding-communities/*.)

Encourage and support a multiplicity of student groups, organizations, teams, and activities. Student activities have value in themselves. They impart actual skills, like singing, debating, sailing, or acting specific to the activity. They nurture the more general interpersonal skills of working with others. They also develop their own symbols, rituals, and traditions. These may be embraced by the entire university community. The student group (its existence and excellence) can itself become a symbol. Alumni are often willing to provide monetary support to continue it.

❑ MIT is well known for its tradition of highly-engineered student pranks (such as putting a police car on the roof of a building). Very few students are actually involved in pranking, but the whole community takes pride in their ingenuity. But just as important to MIT's identity is its tradition of excellence in pistol shooting – and ballroom dancing. Minor sports performed with distinction instill communal pride and counter stereotypes (e.g. these sports counter a stereotype that engineers are all awkward and un-coordinated). The MIT pistol team often triumphs over the U.S. military academies.

❑ Yale has a tradition of a cappella singing groups. Most alumni were not members of a singing group, but such singing groups often perform at reunions, reminding all alumni of that part of the undergraduate culture in which music and performance are valued.

❑ Penn State has a tradition of excellence in football. Other universities take pride in excelling in major sports.

Sometimes traditions and rituals need to be monitored or managed by the university or sponsoring organization so that they develop into nurturing traditions rather than personally destructive ones. Keep things safe.

Institutionalize rites of passage, but make them accessible and revisit-able. Both official and unofficial times of celebration can be turned into memory palaces. However, the intent is not just for alumni (as well as students and their parents) to revisit those times and places in their memories – but for alumni to actually come back and revisit the places in which those rites of passage occurred.

Make pageantry understood by the audience. A convocation for entering students or a graduation exercise are often produced with theatrical pomp and circumstance. However the symbol and gesture from long ago may not be understood by today's students or their parents. Make each song and ceremony relevant. Think about the Parents Parting Ceremony at Morehouse: *http://www.nytimes. com/2015/08/22/us/parents-ceremony-serves-up-elements-of-morehouse-gospel.html?_r=1* .

Memorialize the seasons of youth. Student entertainment, especially when seasonal (such as a winter carnival or spring celebration) or geared to a specific time at university (such as a senior prom) can become concrete memories of time and place. These can be recalled when the seasons turn each year. University team sports can do the same.

Create and preserve spaces to remember. On some campuses, students rub the toe of an iconic statue for good luck. On others, couples may propose marriage under a particular bell tower. In others there are places not just to study, but to grab a cup of coffee, or to sip a glass of wine, or just hang out. If there are not places at university to remember having a special time, no one will remember much of the university. See also 10.3 The Architecture of Return.

Recognize and nurture those traditions that promote university values. Service projects can promote town-gown relations or unite far flung alumni. For example, at Yale, many community service projects are run under the umbrella organization Dwight Hall: *http://dwighthall.org/*. At Penn State, THON is the largest student-run philanthropy in the world, which runs a year-long fundraising effort that culminates in a dance marathon attended by thousands, and viewed on the internet by 150,000: *www.thon.org*. Funds go to fight pediatric cancer.

Extend traditions so that alumni can participate – and not just as spectators or donors. See Chapter 8.2.

For more on traditions, see *http://www.collegexpress.com/lists/list/interesting-college-traditions/765/*, *http://campusgrotto.com/the-100-greatest-college-traditions.html* , *http://www.businessinsider.com/the-best-college-traditions-2014-7?op=1* or *http://fanindex.usatoday.com/2014/11/17/the-10-best-traditions-in-college-football/*. Many universities have a webpage describing their own special traditions.

See 19.1 Preparing Students for a Lifetime of Giving

Chapter 11

Communicating

One of the questions most frequently asked in alumni relations is: what is the best way to use social media? This chapter examines that and other communications issues, but with a certain bias. There is much written in the corporate sphere about communications and social media, where large budgets and expert professionals are devoted exclusively to crafting press releases and other media messages. In contrast, we focus on not-for-profits and volunteer-run organizations with constrained funds, limited personnel, and non-expert volunteers where hard choices must be made. But first, a short comment in which we provide an overview of some of the many (and often bigger budget) items that a large university such as Yale might initiate.

11.1 | University Communications with Alumni

Staying in touch. Yale communicates regularly with over 85% of its 150,000 living alumni by e-mail, letters and materials sent by mail, Twitter, YouTube, iTunes, web sites, and phone calls. Keeping up-to-date with the addresses of alumni is critical to being able to offer and manage the connections and programming Yale provides its alumni. Yale begins this effort even before graduation, with surveys, customized emails, and even gatherings at restaurants and bars near the campus to introduce seniors to those they might be living near after graduation. Yale offers every alumnus and alumna the opportunity to link to an "@aya.yale.edu" email address, that they can keep forever. The opportunity to be listed in Yale's online directory is offered on Yale's web site, where there is a special link for alumni. The Alumni Records Office maintains the University's official alumni database.

News from campus. The Yale Office of Public Affairs and Communications sends a weekly electronic newsletter to all members of the Yale community including alumni for whom it has an e-mail address – Yale News – with current campus news and it also posts a Daily Bulletin online. Yale News and the Daily Bulletin link to stories and YouTube videos, Yale's Flickr account, and other media. The independent Yale Alumni Magazine (YAM) is sent to most alumni for whom Yale has a post office address. YAM contains Yale-connected articles and "Classnotes" – news from Yale College classmates – in each magazine. YAM also has a web site – *www.yalealumnimagazine.com* – and a blog – 06520. In addition, the independent campus newspaper, The Yale Daily News (*www.yaledailynews.com*) publishes on the web and is read by many alumni and parents, in addition to most people on campus.

Multiple points of contact. In addition to news and articles of interest, Yalies receive communications about upcoming programs from their regional organizations, news of classmates from their class, solicitations from their Alumni Fund agent, program information from any shared interest or identity groups to which they belong, communications from Yale Educational Travel, and ballots from the Secretary of the University in connection with the annual election of the Alumni Fellow to the Corporation. In addition to sending e-mails about events, most local clubs and classes and many of the shared interest group organizations also have their own web sites. All of these contacts help keep alumni connected to the University.

11.2 | Effective Use of Social Media for engagement and development

Examples are drawn primarily from the United States, and would have to be adapted for international usage.

White Paper – "Social Media Handbook for Nonprofits – Social Media for Social Good"

Ayelet Baron, a Director of Cisco Systems, compiled 97 pages of useful information from many sources and with many references as well: *http://www.slideshare.net/ayeletb/social-media-for-social-good-1599758* .

Ayelet's white paper covers best practices, what Chief Information Officers should know, where to start, which social media to use, tactics and successes, and how to measure return on investment. Just as importantly, it acknowledges that social media may not be right for everyone – and issues caveats. Written in 2009, some aspects dated, some links broken, but insightful strategic overview. Here is a short extract from the Point of View – Guidelines for Success.

❏ **Don't Do Social Media Just To Do Social Media.** You need to have your website, email marketing and online-fundraising ducks in a row prior to moving into new social-networking space

❏ **Prepare to Lose Control.** If you are not comfortable with this, social networking probably is not for you.

❏ **It's About Two way Communication.** Listen. Social media is not about you. It's about people's relationships with you. Focus on the long term. It takes time to get results and build relationships.

❏ **Dedicate the Right Resources.** Do not hand the responsibility of your social media networks to an intern. Grow or hire an expert.

❏ **Educate Your Leaders.** Before you jump in, make sure that your organization's leaders understand the implications of social media.

Case Study – Election campaigns of Barack Obama

Two of the most successful uses of social media have been the two election campaigns of Barack Obama. They built community, called people to action and raised a lot of money. Much will be written about Obama's 2012 campaign, but case studies have already been written about his earlier 2008 campaign.

The 2008 effort included 5 million supporters on social networks, 50 million viewers of campaign-related YouTube videos, 1 billion e-mails, over 100 thousand Twitter followers, and 6.5 million online donations totaling more than $500 million, with 6 million of them of $100 or less. For a short readable overview, with useful details concerning some specific social media strategies for developing community and raising funds, see the European Business Review: "Obama and the power of social media and technology," by Jennifer Aaker and Victoria Chang: *http://faculty-gsb.stanford.edu/aaker/pages/documents/TEBRMay-June-Obama.pdf* .

A short introduction – some social media strategies, tools, and tactics from Kaukab Jhumra Smith

- *http://smartblogs.com/social-media/2010/08/13/how-to-raise-funds-for-your-nonprofit-using-social-media/*
- Figure out where your prospective donors are [including where they are online]. It comes back to the same basic social-media commandment: Listen first to find your people.
- Bring it down to one person's story.
- Demonstrate your impact.
- Create a personal connection through video.
- Use mobile messaging – Texted donations work best when your donors are already primed to act because of all the work you'd done beforehand through e-mail and other communication.

See SmartBlogs, "How to raise funds for your nonprofit using social media:"

- *http://smartblogs.com/social-media/2010/08/13/how-to-raise-funds-for-your-nonprofit-using-social-media/*.

An innovative online campaign with "game-like" features.

The volunteer-based alumni association of SSE-Riga pushed annual contribution rates from 11% to 33% with an online fundraising campaign: *https://vimeo.com/52150696* . Instantaneous feedback and multiple rankings harnessed the competitive spirit of their business-oriented alumni.

11.3 | When Volunteers manage and maintain media

Electronic media have made communication easier. Sometimes easier than we would like, but often not as easy as we think.

Create what is essential – for the rest, go with the flow. Control and create the essential messages that must be delivered. Allow – and even promote – appropriate optional elaboration. Volunteers do not always have the time or bandwidth to meet specific deadlines, or create the high message flow espoused by social media gurus. But whatever content is produced will carry weight with those that follow the content creator.

If you can't let go – at least loosen your grip. You can only control the content you create. You do not even have the resources to create all the content that you need to engage alumni. Besides, you can no longer stop people from creating content and publishing it to the world.

Create safe and simple playgrounds – or support them. The difficulty of providing and maintaining secure university servers, development environments, and creation tools is tremendous. The expense is enormous, but justified for official university branded content. However, these things are available for free (or almost for free) on the internet. (No university can control Facebook, or even Linked-In.) It benefits the university to support – or even provide – "free" but mentored places in the Cloud for non-branded and lightly-branded alumni-related content. This can be done inexpensively. It also means that alumni-created content will not be lost when alumni die or stop a paid service. It even means that content will not be lost when the University IT budget is axed.

Engage alumni artists, coders, and writers. Members of this group are often overlooked by the university unless they become rich and famous. They may also be the type of people who do not work well in the committee-style projects of many alumni organizations. Yet they can be energetic, intense, and creative. Electronic media is a vehicle to involve them. They may be short on treasure, but rich in time and talent.

Everyone has different tastes – respect them. Everyone has different eyes and sees differently. Everyone has different ears and hears differently. Tolerate vision and voice (visual and textual content styles) that are different than yours – better yet, support those styles that resonate with the intended audience of club, class, or affinity group.

Don't rely exclusively on Facebook – do understand WordPress and Blogger. Social Media companies such as Facebook and LinkedIn are in flux trying to monetize their eyeballs, which means that their policies have been and are likely to change. (For example, the changing definition of a Facebook "group" has destroyed some online communities.) This can seriously impact the reliability of the "free" part of their messaging. It has been said that only 16% of the people who like a Facebook page see any given post. Nonetheless some people and organizations rely on a Facebook page as the primary online presence. In contrast, WordPress and Blogger were designed for the slower pace of blogs, but have morphed into tools for creating websites. It is said that 1/5 of all websites are created with WordPress.

Blogger is a proprietary free service provided by Google, but tied to a particular user's Google account. A long-term issue for a website based on Blogger may be transferring the site to another webmaster, especially when change is sudden. A similar free (but advertising supported) service is available through WordPress.com. An upgrade (for a fee) will remove advertising. WordPress.org is free open-source software than can be installed on any server; it allows greater control than WordPress.com. An organization can purchase low-cost hosting contracts from companies such as GoDaddy.com. Many of these hosting contracts include "one-click" installation of multiple instances of WordPress. Services may be priced on an a-la-cart basis, but are much less than a university's IT infrastructure.

Understand "cobbleware" and know when it is appropriate. You can "cobble" together a variety of low cost or free services for not-for-profit organizations, if they require little bandwidth or through put. This "cobbleware" is reliable within its limits, so may suit small components of a volunteer alumni organization. They may not be suitable for volunteer organizations that have sufficient funds to pay for more robust IT solutions and the maintenance thereof.

11.4 | Planning Multiple-Location Events using social media

One way to involve many alumni in a "single" event and leverage volunteer efforts is to have it distributed over a number of sites. The events have to be fun or tap into an emotion. An existing student tradition can go "global" – or with annual repetition, a new alumni tradition can be created. Multi-location events are a way to "cross-pollinate" among existing organizations such as regional chapters and they can be a way to build a new organization based on alumni interests. *The "single" event can even be distributed over time using a number of different dates.*

Participants feel like they are part of a larger effort or happening closely connected to the university. Even a small group of five to ten people will feel the connection if they know that their event is part of a much larger event or effort. A multi-location event can significantly help small regional associations (or local chapters of shared interest groups) with programming by providing an additional event that is closely associated with the university – with little cost to the university or the local groups. *Social media can also be used during and after the event(s) to "tie" them together.*

Examples of global distributed activities and international multi-location events.

❑ **Traditional sports rivalries.** Attending television broadcasts of athletic contests between traditional university rivals has often been the impetus for local gatherings. Planning a local event is eased because the date of the contest is set well in advance and publicized widely by the broadcaster as well as by the university. In many cases, the contest can be viewed at a local sports bar – lowering venue overhead. Publicizing time and location of local events (often by a local alumni association) is still necessary. Ideally, a central web presence publicizes local venues to increase turnout. Examples include "The Game" between Yale and Harvard in late November or The Boat Race between Oxford and Cambridge in March.

❑ **Feb Club Emeritus.** Feb Club was originally a series of Yale undergraduate student social events to enliven the coldest, dampest month of the year – February – by holding a party at Yale every night of the month. However, since 2008, it has become an annual social event for alumni around the world (*www.febclub.webs.com*). As an alumni tradition the proclaimed intent is to hold an alumni get-together (no matter how small) somewhere in the world every night of February. To have an "official" event, all you need is a volunteer "host" at a local pub, where alumni can meet with little or no preparation. Alums can pay for their own drinks, so there is no cost to the host or regional association. More elaborate events are also held by those with time or money to do it. There are currently over 100 Feb Club events around the globe attended by over 5000 alumni.

❑ **Yale Day of Service.** The Yale Day of Service (DoS) (*www.yaledayofservice.org*) was begun in 2008 to tap into Yale's student traditions of community service and social justice. Every year, the second Saturday of May is designated as the Yale DoS. On that day (or as close to that day as possible), alumni and their families and friends volunteer their time to a local community organization for a service program such as park clean-up, tutoring or mentoring. The effort involves over 4000 Yale alumni, family and friends at over 250 sites around the world. Many DoS projects are part of ongoing efforts by local Yale Clubs or other Yale alumni organizations.

Centralized planning with local execution ensures a well-organized event that reflects the interests of a wide array of alumni. However, success often requires some of the characteristics of a successful flash mob or message that has gone viral. For each event, there need to be clear instructions defining participation that allows significant local flexibility; the structure should allow volunteers to self-organize each event without central control; the university must provide centralized online sign ups and automatic email reminders, and built in social media sharing.

Building and maintaining distributed events usually requires an online framework for local implementation. It can be useful for both organizers and participants to be able to sign up through the system. Both Feb Club and DoS encourage individual site organizers to sign up – not just regional associations – in addition to the individual participants. This allows Shared Interest Groups and even a group of friends to participate with their own event.

Feb Club Emeritus was organized from the bottom up by a few alumni volunteers. It spread virally as a fun and unique Yale tradition. However, the simple centralized online framework has allowed it to continue and grow. In contrast, Yale DoS was a concerted effort organized by AYA from the top down including the creation of a volunteer leadership structure. But the flexibility for participation has allowed a simple centralized online framework with regional coordinators to support continued growth from the bottom up.

See also 19.2 Keeping the Connection with young alumni

 PART III

ORGANIZATIONS AND THEIR PLANNED EVENTS

The main organizations of alumni efforts at Yale were described in Part I: Classes, Clubs, Graduate and Professional Schools, Shared Interest Groups (SIGs), and Service Initiatives. This section details how volunteer efforts are used by these entities to plan and undertake programs and events.

For some readers, the information might be more helpful based on the type of event, rather than the type of organization staging the event. Certain types of events are most often organized by certain types of alumni organizations. So chapters of this section can also be characterized as focusing on types of events.

Here is how this section pairs alumni organizations with types of events.

❏ Classes stage reunions;

❏ Chapters (also called clubs or regional associations) plan local events;

❏ Graduate and Professional Schools hold convocations and colloquia (while some may stage class reunions, they are just as likely to hold school-wide convocations, department-specific symposia, or regional gatherings);

❏ SIGs stage thematic conferences at the national and international level, although they are also like (and work with) regional associations at a local level;

❏ Service Initiatives produce service-oriented travel and multi-locational service opportunities (among other things).

Consequently each of the chapters in this section of the Guide serves a dual purpose – detailing how volunteers successfully accomplish events within an organization type, and how volunteers plan the programs that a specific alumni organization undertakes.

Chapter 12

Classes
(Reunions and Homecomings)

Classes were the first alumni group to self-organize – over two hundred years ago. Their main project is Class reunions.

School reunions are deeply ingrained in American culture. They are prevalent at colleges and universities and also high schools. (The United States has well over 2,500 colleges and universities offering 4 year degree granting programs, and well over 30,000 high schools.) Class reunions are common (*https://en.wikipedia.org/wiki/Class_reunion*), as are alumni weekends (a school-wide reunion) and homecomings (*https://en.wikipedia.org/wiki/Homecoming*). Sometimes school-wide alumni weekends include special Class celebrations. Homecomings, at least in high schools, are often associated with school football team athletic events in the fall season. The homecoming is included as part of festivities at a particular football game, perhaps with an arch-rival or perhaps the last "home" football game of the year. These homecomings may have separate student and alumni events. Some schools have both fall homecoming and spring or summer class reunion events.

Certainly, staying in touch is important to members of Classes – and that self-interest is what originally drove that self-organization. Today, they stay in touch by many means, including newsletters, class notes, Facebook pages, blogs, listservs, and web pages. Undoubtedly some younger classes are using social media such as Instagram, Pinterest, or Twitter. While staying in touch may have once been difficult, it no longer is. Fundraising is also undertaken in the context of the Class cohort and on behalf of Classes. However, the major organizational projects that Classes undertake are Class Reunions when they return to their alma mater.

Often (and certainly at Yale) Class volunteers are helped in the planning and execution of these on-campus gatherings by university alumni relations departments and their professionals. This chapter will detail some of the considerations in planning a successful reunion.

As with any volunteer organization, Classes face issues of recruiting volunteers, engaging them, and cultivating volunteers. For reunion purposes, these efforts are sporadic, often just during a Reunion planning cycle of a year or two. Nonetheless, the principles for recruiting volunteers, engaging them, and cultivating leaders that are described in Part II are relevant here as well. Most Classes contain subgroups based upon the undergraduate activities, interests, identities and passions in which they engaged as students. Volunteers from an affinity group within a Class can solicit attendance at the reunion and can organize reunion activities for their affinity group. The occasion of the Class reunion provides an opportunity for an affinity group within a Class such as singers or athletes to organize itself in conjunction with or in a way similar to larger university-wide affinity groups as discussed in Part II.

Some Classes have smaller mini-reunions or regional gatherings, and groups of classmates may participate in other class specific activities, but these are much smaller events. For additional information about mini-reunions see *www.yalegale.org/casestudies* . In addition graduate and professional schools as well as many shared interest groups (SIGs or affinity groups) also plan reunions that generally cross age cohorts, whether at university or elsewhere. Similar considerations for planning a successful SIG reunion apply.

12.1 | Reunions
planning a successful reunion – part 1

Whether your organization already runs a robust reunion program or whether you are planning your first ever reunion, the steps below will focus your efforts and help you to plan a successful and productive reunion.

Step 1: Determine Your Objectives. You likely have many goals for your reunion celebration, and a reunion, especially in the form of a multi-day reunion weekend, can deliver on many goals simultaneously. You want to determine at the outset which goals are most important and reflect those goals in your programming. Some programming may be created specifically to foster these goals.

- What do you want to accomplish with your reunion?
- Is the primary objective to bring people together to reconnect with one another?
- Is the primary objective for alumni to reconnect with the university?
- Are you celebrating the accomplishments of certain individuals?
- Are you attempting to show alumni how the university has changed since they attended?
- Are you trying to raise donations for a specific endeavor?
- Is there a theme or life concern that you want to discuss with a specific group of alumni?

Step 2: Determine Your Audience. Knowing your objectives will help you decide if you should plan Class reunions or a Homecoming or another type of reunion depending on your target audience such as young alumni, older alumni, alumni sharing a specific interest, or all alumni. The typical American model (which Yale initiated) is to have a class reunion every five years (bring classes back 5, 10, 15, etc. years after graduation) to maintain the basic connection to the university established when they were students. Not all schools follow this model however. Some schools (Princeton) invite alumni to return every year although they put special emphasis on the five year classes for the annual reunion weekend.

A key question is how many segments of the alumni population will you invite (ten classes, twenty classes, one area of study or more) and how many alumni do you expect will attend? Many schools enjoying larger attendance (Yale included) have most of the reunion events organized as class or interest group specific activities even when they are on campus the same day or weekend. Other schools (and programs) will run most of their programming as one large group with one or two events that breakout by cohort. Each approach has its benefits such as strengthening class ties or networking between classes though the logistics involved in your program may ultimately determine your decision. For a discussion about audience see *http://www.iup.edu/upper.aspx?id=88431*.

Step 3: Find a Venue / Related Impact on Scheduling and Logistics. Venue is a crucial decision deeply linked to scheduling and logistics. Organizing at your university provides access to university resources such as faculty lecturers, classroom facilities, and experienced event planners as well as the ability to tap into university traditions such as athletic events and graduations but is constrained by the academic schedule and the need of the student body for the facilities. An interesting venue not on or near campus maybe be an attraction as a destination in its own right, especially for a smaller group or on an off-cycle year (like Yale's mini- reunions). Off campus events often rely more on volunteers and less on university staff for logistics. For choosing venues: *http://www.military.com/Resources/ResourceSubmittedFileView?file=reunions_how_to_plan.htm* .

Step 4: Schedule the Event. For a large event, the University itself often schedules dates, and is deeply involved in planning sub-events. Some universities have traditional Homecoming or Alumni weekends during which the University will assist smaller groups that wish to hold their own reunion. *http://www.iup.edu/upper.aspx?id=88431*, *http://alumni.dal.ca/get-connected/dal-homecoming/reunions/reunion-planning-guide/*.

Step 5: Logistics. Depending on your institution, there may (or may not) be resources available to support the logistical planning involved in a reunion. There is a great deal of event planning (booking spaces, planning meals and lodging, accepting RSVPS and payment) and if the university is not able to provide resources to assist with this aspect of the reunion, your class or volunteer group may want to consider hiring a professional event planner.

12.2 | Reunions
planning a successful reunion – part 2

So you've decided on your objectives, your audience, your venue, your dates, and who is doing logistics. Or those have been determined by university tradition. What are the next steps in planning a particular reunion or event?

Step 1: Build Your Volunteer Team. Building a strong leadership team for each reunion is extremely important. Not only will the leadership team help you to set your goals and plan your events, they will be in the forefront of your attendance efforts. You have heard it before: the more passionate leaders involved, the more alumni that are likely to get involved and attend! Although you'll utilize many communication vehicles including email, regular mail, web pages and social media tools such as the organization's Facebook page to get your message out, the most successful reunion outreach is always one-to-one. A robust and active reunion committee can make all the difference in getting others to attend.

Step 2: Add Customized Meaningful Content. Most robust reunion programs contain several social events such as cocktail parties or dinners, lectures by professors, panels by notable alumni and addresses by university administrators, often the President. What is often most meaningful to participants, however, are the unique aspects that the alumni leadership creates. Whether publishing a class book, including alumni panels focused on group specific issues (such as raising children or retiring from careers), including performances highlighting the group talent (whether in art, music, film or other areas) or even including a well-executed memorial service for deceased friends. The unique events or activities that the volunteer organizers put together often develop from ideas from the volunteer team and may at first seem odd, but should be nurtured and supported.

Step 3: Execute the Plan. Reunion should be fun! It should be enjoyable for both the alumni attending and the volunteer group that organized the weekend. Volunteer leaders especially, as organizers, should plan for the fun (whether by including certain surprises or celebratory events) and have an active role in leading the excitement especially if they sense that the group dynamic is not developing. While managing the last minute details can be a distraction, volunteers should take some time to make sure that the feel of the event is what they intended. Attendees are going to want to speak with the organizers and the leadership team so it's important for volunteer leaders to circulate and make sure everyone is comfortable.

Step 4: Continuing the Momentum. People generally leave a reunion inspired about their organization and the university. To build on the interest, you should incorporate ideas for continued involvement with the university into your communications and programming. After the reunion, in the communications that thank the participants and especially the volunteer leadership, you have the opportunity to build on the momentum from the reunion and help to strengthen the alumni engagement with the university.

Additional resources and ideas. Here are some links.

- *http://dartmouth.org/reunionplanning/* , *http://www.military.com/Resources/ResourceSubmittedFileView?file=reunions_how_to_plan.htm*

- *http://www.iup.edu/alumni/visit/tours/*

- *http://alumni.dal.ca/get-connected/dal-homecoming/reunions/reunion-planning-guide/* , *http://www.reunionsmag.com/resources/resources_FreeStuff.html*

- *http://www.case.org/Browse_by_Professional_Interest/Special_Events/Homecoming_and_Reunions.html* (public index of articles, access to an individual article requires password)

For sample Yale Class Reunion Schedules see *www.yalegale.org/resources/wp-content/uploads/2014/12/Reunion_schedules.pdf* . This details, in a side by side comparison, the 2014 Class Reunion programming for two Classes – the Class of 1974 and the Class of 2004.

12.3 | Volunteer-run Reunions from the professional's view

At Yale every graduating class holds a reunion on campus every 5 years. Several professionals at the Association of Yale Alumni work primarily with Classes (the groups of students who graduated from the College in a specific year). Each professional usually works the same reunions each year, for example, the 40th, the 45th, the 50th and the 55th. Each Yale College Reunion is planned in partnership with between one and three volunteer reunion chairs who are appointed by their class secretary (or what might be called their class "president"). While the reunions themselves vary greatly in character, there are some common principles that govern the way AYA shepherds reunion chairs through the reunion planning process.

Here are some best practices and logistical concerns that you might keep in mind.

Train your volunteers well. Reunions can be very complex and involve a number of different deadlines for tasks ranging from communications to budget building to decisions about menus. AYA helps reunion chairs get their minds around this complexity in two ways: by inviting them to a day-long Reunion Chairs Workshop nine months in advance, and by providing them with a binder full of information and a planning calendar, to keep them on track in the following months.

Share information about past reunions. Reunion chairs are always invited to attend the corresponding reunion the year preceding their own gathering in New Haven. They also have access to the printed programs of several previous reunions. From this kind of exposure to what classes have done before them, reunion chairs can make informed decisions about what might work best for their class.

Stay in constant touch. Staying in touch with reunion chairs and their committees is very important. The best ways to do so may depend on the age group with which you are working. For some professionals at AYA, the most frequent correspondence with chairs is by email. For professionals working with older alumni the most frequent method may be by telephone. Some get reunion chairs and committees together by conference call on a periodic basis. Staying informed about what your chairs are planning helps prevent misunderstandings and even disaster. You may spend a significant amount of time writing emails explaining why something will or will not work. Your steady and encouraging advice will be the key to their success.

Leave the details to professionals. If your budget permits it, make sure that the logistics of a reunion are overseen by professionals. This means not just alumni relations professionals, but also caterers, tent companies, furniture rental companies, sound and lighting technicians, and the like. Yale handles the cost of these vendor services by charging each class a flat per-person price. When university alumni relations professionals have long-term relationships with the reunion vendors (both on and off campus ones), the university professionals can negotiate more effectively than volunteers who may work with this vendor only once in a lifetime. This is also important because the university may be the one ultimately paying the bill.

Encourage creativity. While much of your job will be to manage your reunion chairs, and to make sure that the logistics of the reunion run smoothly, don't be too quick to dismiss a creative idea. This may be a desire to expand or adapt what some other class did, or to try something entirely new.

Show your appreciation. In addition to thanking your reunion chairs throughout the planning process, consider some kind of gesture during the reunion itself, or afterwards. For example, AYA offers reunion chairs accommodations in a guest suite on-campus at their reunion headquarters. This allows them to be close to the action but still enjoy the comforts of air-conditioning and other amenities. On the day a reunion chair arrives for the reunion, AYA has a box of locally baked gourmet cookies ready for them; and sometime during the summer following the reunion the Executive Director sends each reunion chair a thank you letter accompanied by a modest gift.

12.4 | Building Attendance at a Reunion
the art of the invitation

Publicizing a reunion is essential, but not enough to draw strong attendance. Just like a party or wedding, people want to get the formal invitation and the personal invite. They want to know that they are welcome, that they will know the other guests, and that they will enjoy themselves enough to justify the time and expense of participating.

Issue the formal invitation. Use snail mail for a "Save-the-Date" postcard, then later the formal invitation. (It has higher impact than email or other electronic media.) Back them up with email notices. When appropriate, snail mail missives should request email addresses for future emails. It's a good way to gather and update contact information.

Personalize it. The more personal the invitation, the more persuasive. The most compelling is made face-to-face by a friend. Next is a phone call – from someone you know. Then a written invitation personalized just for you. Blast emails and public notices are much less effective. That's why attendance committees that personally contact as many potential reunion attendees as possible are so important. Effective efforts to boost attendance take a lot of work. See also *http://aya.yale.edu/content/attendance-building-basics* .

How do you maximize opportunities for face-to-face invitations? Create a series of pre-reunion events throughout the key regions where most invitees live. Ask local enthusiasts to help organize and host events in the many regions where potential attendees are concentrated or scattered. Hosts need to help guests enjoy the event AND invite each guest to the reunion – and everyone must enjoy the event enough to want to do it again by coming to reunion. A by-product is that each event creates multiple points of communications (see below): announcing each event and then reporting on the fun everyone had at it.

How do you maximize opportunities for one-to-one verbal invitations? Appoint an Attendance Committee, whose job includes contacting as many invitees – one-to-one – as possible.

❏ **Attendance Committees need to be large.** Remember the phone tree rule of thumb: each person should only have to telephone 5 to 8 other people. See *http://www.aauw.org/ resource/how-to-build-a-phone-tree/*.

❏ **Attendance Committees need to be diverse.** If you include just your friends, you will only phone each other. Instead, include someone (or two or three) from every sports team to phone members of that team. Include representatives from every singing group, orchestra, marching band, drama society, improvisation group, debating club, student political association, dance troop, religious society, fraternity, sorority, student newspaper, literary magazine, humor publication, ethnic cultural center, student government, honor society, social service organization, residential dormitory ... the list goes on. The value of a university supporting many student groups is not only that they enrich the students' life while at university, but also that they provide a way to connect with them once they have left. Remember that alumni might not give contact information to the university, but their friends and teammates still know how to reach them.

❏ **Student phone banks.** Phone calls from people outside the reunion guest list are much less effective. However, alumni will often politely take calls from students – especially if they are not being asked for money. In addition, the cost of student phone banks may be much less than a commercial operation.

❏ **Recorded phone-trees.** Everyone hates incessant robo-calls. However, a few short, select and well-thought-out recorded messages may be useful. A short recorded call from a famous classmate may produce good results. So may one from the class treasurer saying he's not asking for dues, just asking you to join the fun. For additional information see *https://www.callfire.com/ help/glossary/communications/phone-tree* .

Repeat it. Reinforce the invitation – and the message of community – through repetition. Tell people to "save the date" long before the actual invitation – then later send out reminders. Plan the basic timeline for contacting people long before the event – have a timeline in place at least a year ahead. Include the date of each specific communication, the type of media (e.g. phone, email, alumni magazine), the deadline for creating it and who is responsible for the creation and delivery. Using multiple media channels strengthens and deepens the message.

Remember, building attendance is work, but it should be fun too. It's a good opportunity to talk with old friends.

See 6.2 The 40th Reunion of the Class of 1970 — a case study in volunteer engagement

See 13.1.1 Engaging Alumni of Different Ages

Chapter 13

Clubs and Chapters (Regional Programs)

Alumni Clubs (known elsewhere as regional associations, circles, chapters, or networks) were the second type of Yale alumni group to self-organize, 150 years ago. Their main projects are local to the organization – and usually far from the Yale campus.

In some instances, universities have the resources to help regional associations with organizational matters and events. However, in many cases regional associations are left to their own devices. They often rely exclusively on local alumni volunteers. Regional associations apply the precepts of Part II on organizing volunteer communities all the time.

Some regional associations assess dues. Some of the larger ones are able to hire their own staff (even if part time). However, many of the smaller or more dispersed chapters rely almost exclusively on self-funded events and volunteers, where attendees pay their share of the cost of the event.

Some regional associations partner with local chapters of shared interest groups in organizing events and publicize local SIG events. Some chapters take on a more central role and act as a facilitator for the formation of SIG groups and events within their ranks. This allows the association to provide broader programming to regional alumni through the SIG volunteers, and provides a broader and larger audience (when appropriate) for SIG programming.

This chapter will look at programming events for a regional association as well as how local alumni can help provide internships and mentoring to current university students – and much of this will apply to a regional chapter of a SIG. The chapter will also look at regional associations that are in another country from the alma mater – and some of the specific problems that they face.

13.1 | Programs to Sustain Alumni Engagement

Programming for your audience. Know your audience. Learn what they like. The geographic region and the urban, suburban or rural nature of the locale affect what works. The age of the intended audience does too. So does the cost.

The best way to know what events are of interest is to solicit programming suggestions from alumni and members by a simple survey (*http://aya.yale.edu/content/membership-surveys_1570* ; *www.surveymonkey.com*) or social media. Segment your audience so each person can respond with the most comfortable tool whether paper-and-pencil or on-line.

Programming for your resources. Know your group limitations and resources. Planning an event requires volunteer time, talent, and, sometimes, treasure or financial capacity. The essential resource is the leadership of volunteers who are committed, willing and able to plan, organize, and produce an event. Financial resources in an association's accounts or funds generated by an event should be of secondary importance.

❑ Leadership, whether professional or volunteer, should encourage event planners to produce events that they are enthusiastic about producing and have the capabilities to produce and execute with excellence.

❑ Look for reproducible events. The necessary effort for the subsequent event will be reduced, even if the event grows in size. Some can be made reproducible by altering them slightly to fit the resources available. For example, an association can hold a reception every year for local students who have graduated from high school, been accepted by the University and will be attending the University the next year.

❑ Small or large events are only successful, if within the budget for time, talent and treasure.

❑ The size of the event or the amount of financial investment is not determinative of the interest or fun generated. Small groups, even one or two people, can produce fun and interesting events.

Creating program-ready traditions. Build events around institutional traditions and annual events to strengthen alumni participation. Coordinating around an existing university event can be an opportunity for a relatively easy and inexpensive get-together with continuing appeal to successive generations of alumni.

❑ Take a few existing student traditions and reshape and repurpose them as alumni events. See for example, Feb Club (Chapter 3.2.3). Sometimes this entails the alumni relations professionals helping to shape and promote select student traditions, so that they will have continuing appeal as students become alumni. Otherwise, alumni relations professionals and volunteers around campus can be instrumental in creating student traditions.

❑ Have an annual party at a time during the year that is usually vacant on the social calendar, like Feb Club (see Chapter 3.2.3).

❑ Organize a community service tradition that can get people outside, like Day of Service (see Chapter 3.5.1).

❑ Take advantage of a spectator sports event or inter-university rivalry such as the Harvard-Yale Football Game (*http://aya.yale.edu/content/yaleharvard-game*).

❑ Build on a seasonal University event or need (college fairs in the U.S. or interviewing high school students applying to university for admission: Yale Alumni Schools Committee: see Chapter 4).

Creating low-cost, easy-to-organize university-branded programming.

❑ Identify professors who give accessible lectures of their current research then take the show on the road by paying their travel expenses (within limits of financial and organizational resources): AYA-Redpath Speakers Program (*http://aya.yale.edu/content/speakers-program*).

❑ The University or alumni associations can work together with publicists to monitor the travels of University connected people. Many authors, playwrights, musicians, artists, and professors tour to promote their work, or give promotional talks. Local associations can plan an event to coordinate with a regional visit, such as a presentation and luncheon.

Resources for ideas on a wide variety of events.

❑ A sample list of events categorized by audience: see Chapter 13.1.2 below.

❑ Suggested themes, venues, and talent sources: *http://aya.yale.edu/content/advice-examples* .

❑ Events sponsored by the Yale Club of Washington, DC, a large association not located near Yale: *http://www.yaleclubdc.org/event-calendar* .

❑ Events organized by a smaller club with a scattered alumni base, the Yale Club of Central Pennsylvania that might have only a handful of events every year: *www.PaYale.com* .

A shorter list of events with more detail about each event including the resources needed to hold it and instructions for making it happen: *www.yalegale.org/casestudies* .

13.1.1 | Engaging Alumni of Different Ages

Universities used to take a one size fits all approach to their alumni events. They held reunions, arranged professorial lectures, and scheduled formal dinners. However, many now realize that different kinds of events, tailored to different specific age groups, can be quite successful. Some such events gain a life of their own that extends beyond their niche. Targeted programming also helps make those events that bridge age differences all the more special and meaningful.

What has worked for Yale alumni organizations? Many of Yale's regional associations have been segmenting their activities by age for some time (see *http://aya.yale.edu/content/advice-examples*). These regional clubs have found the following distinct needs for varying age groups and have developed programs to successfully address these needs.

❑ **Younger alumni** want ongoing informal networking, are career focused, and have significant after-work free time. Examples: A regular once-a-month get together that rotates location such as among various bars or restaurants (social focus) / networking events (career focus) / wine or cheese tastings / ongoing weeknight service activities.

❑ **Alumni with young families** experience time crunch between work and family, prefer activities limited to weekends (evening activities interfere with bedtime routines), want value-focused activities (both in terms of ideals and in terms of cost), and desire activities that repeat and create a sense of tradition for their children. Examples: Day of Service activities, holiday parties, summer picnics, telecasts of Yale-Harvard athletic contests.

❑ **Older alumni** experience a desire to learn or re-learn, expect quality programming, have evening weeknights often available. Examples: traditional lectures with dinner receptions, continuing-education-type classes, lectures on the deeper meaning of life.

Note: creating activities to appeal to a particular age group does not mean other age groups should be prohibited from attending. Often, as is the case with the Day of Service, an activity has a natural appeal to many age groups and/or can grow to include many age groups. Even within these guidelines, there will be regional and cultural variations.

How do you find out what might work for your organization? Just ask! Seek ideas for age appropriate events via focus groups, surveys, or just by talking to alumni from different particular age groups. Do not merely ask them what they would like you to do. Ask them what events they would like to run for their friends. Offer to help accomplish their goals. Then you have some volunteers to help organize and run the event – and promote it to their friends.

How do you recruit alumni volunteers of different ages and empower them to work on programming? Recruiting volunteers of different age groups happens naturally for Class Reunions (which are based on age cohort). However, some believe this is more difficult for general all-school homecomings, regional associations, or shared interest groups.

❑ **Keep up-to-date lists of alumni and help constituent organizations manage their own lists.** Where permitted (and legal) send the appropriate list to the chapters, regional organizations, shared interest groups, and other constituent organizations. Otherwise be willing to send out invitations and information for the constituent organizations. Information technology can update lists automatically, but only if the university (or central office of the alumni organization) keeps good electronic records. Lists should be updated when students graduate (and become alumni) and when alumni move. Have a contact number and person at the central office, where chapters and regional organizations can report a move (or death).

❑ **Welcome new alumni** and those alumni new to a region. This does much to foster interest and volunteerism. It is just as important to listen to them, and support their efforts when they do volunteer.

❑ **Thank your volunteers.** And thank them again, regardless of age. This simply cannot be stressed enough.

Alumni organizations can use their Board of Directors to promote volunteer leadership – by requiring each Board member to organize and run an activity or two every year. By including representatives from all age groups on the Board of Directors and requiring all members of the Board to organize an event, you also build a pipeline of events for each age cohort. (This applies whether the organization is national, regional, or a Shared Interest Group.) Look for that spark of interest and impact in participants and seek to foster it. Making service to the organization meaningful and fun keeps volunteers active.

If an organization is committed to having activities for different ages, reaching out and gathering opinions as to what those activities might be should uncover great ideas and the individuals willing to spearhead those ideas.

13.1.2 | List of sample regional association activities

Educational Opportunities
- Lectures, panels on academic, political, health, or social issues
- Study groups on topical issues
- Educational tours organized and sponsored by regional association

Social and Networking Activities
- All age groups
  - Spectator sports: attendance at university, or regional and local amateur and professional sporting events
  - Picnics
  - Historical tours: museums, art galleries, historical sites
  - Professional or career building information events such as networking
  - Dinners/luncheon with programs
  - Career nights for professional networking
  - Job banks with positions offered by alumni/alumnae of the university associated with the regional association
  - Career mentoring
- Recent and young alumni/alumnae
  - Cocktail parties
  - Theater or musical outings
  - Participatory activities
    - Sports teams sponsored by the regional association in inter-association leagues
    - Dancing
  - Wine Tours
- Middle age to senior alumni/alumnae
  - Health related discussions and symposia
  - Financial and retirement planning offerings

- Singles events
- Young families
    - Children's book readings
    - Children's age appropriate events
        - Art related
        - Cooking with parents
    - Outings: picnics, amusement parks
- Alumni-student (mixed age) activities
    - Lunches, dinners or other programs during student holidays or breaks
    - Alumni mentoring, or help with job interview or search techniques
    - Summer internships, including association social activities for alumni and interns sponsored by the association

Service Offerings

- Regular service or charitable events
    - Sponsored by regional association on a repeating basis
    - Sponsored by non-association NGOs on repeating basis
- Special or theme organized days of service with community NGOs including charities
- Educational mentoring – this is also representing the university
    - Tutoring local students, even if not candidates for the university
    - Mentoring students about general university application processes.

Continued Connection with the University

- Events, meetings, talks by university officials on the state of the university and other developments
- Representing the university at events where students learn about different universities
- Lectures by university professors or researchers, "subsidized" by university

13.2 | Student Internships, Mentoring and alumni participation

An internship is essentially short-term on-the-job training in a field that a student or young worker wants to learn more about. There are also research internships, more common in scientific fields, in which a higher-level student examines a particular topic on behalf of a business before producing a written study or presentation.

Internship Advantages. Internships provide value to both the intern and the employer.

For the intern. For-profit corporations and not-for-profit organizations across America provide a wide range of internship opportunities during the summer and other vacations for students. From an intern's standpoint, this is an opportunity to gain a first-hand perspective on real-world problem-solving – applying class room theory to actual situations requiring practical solutions. It can also be an opportunity to demonstrate to a potential employer one's effectiveness on the job. In some ways, it is like a long interview – for the intern to assess interest in the organization.

For the employer. The employer has an opportunity to "sell" the company to a talented student who might later become an employee. Of course, these internships also provide the employer with the benefit of a "long interview" with prospective employees. It is not unusual for employers to extend offers for full-time employment to interns on completion of their assignments. In addition, an employer can use interns to start a special project (even if it is not completed). The employer can benefit significantly from the intern's fresh ideas unencumbered by any traditional organizational impediments. Having very intelligent, high energy, willing interns who are available at modest or no cost to undertake a project can prove to be very attractive to employers.

Issues and opportunities. An effective internship program requires having leadership and supervision in place to ensure that the intern is supervised responsibly, has a well-defined role and can gain meaningful guidance and feedback on an ongoing basis. If appropriate leadership is in place, it is worth considering a program that employs multiple interns thereby creating a social structure within the program. If appropriate leadership is not available, then an internship should not be offered.

Alumni can be very helpful in identifying internship opportunities. In many cases, alumni themselves can utilize the capabilities of an intern under their own supervision or within their organization. This is ideal because it provides a meaningful and productive experience for the alumnus as well as serving the interest of the intern and of the University.

Mentoring. Alumni involvement as mentors for students can be quite meaningful and beneficial. Offering opportunities to "shadow" an alumnus or alumna during the course of a typical work day affords the student a first-hand experience in what it is like to address key decision-making situations on a real-time basis.

Outside of an organizational setting, alumni can fill a gap in underserved segments of the population where young students lack effective role models. Students who come from divorced families, or come from circumstances where no family member has ever gone to college or provided such a role model, can benefit greatly from alumni who are willing to invest themselves as role models and mentors. Mentoring activities can prove to be enlightening both for mentees and mentors. Alumni sharing life experiences in preparing to go to college, contemplating a career direction and establishing a family are invaluable to students and rewarding for mentors. It is motivating and affirming to mentees to discover that many successful mentors came from modest circumstances and overcame many economic and emotional challenges.

In sum. Alumni find extending a helping hand to young people a rewarding experience especially where the young people are in need of opportunities to advance themselves. Providing internships, or simply assisting such youth in the discovery of how successful people achieve their success, can be quite rewarding for all.

13.2.1 | Creating a "Bulldogs" Intern Program

Introducing students to new employment markets and opportunities. In large cities and within many large companies, there are well developed internship programs offering opportunities to students. In mid-size cities or for smaller companies, local alumni-driven internship programs can provide the crucial connection to students and the university. Alumni within a community can identify internships and communicate about them with the university – or be the conduit for offering interns to employers that realize the availability of qualified interns.

Many universities have a career office that helps to organize internships and other vacation time programs for students as well as assisting in career placement at graduation. At Yale, there is a program that specifically focuses on promoting clusters of internships in small to mid-size cities – which at the same time creates both a strong social component among the interns as well as career-building work experiences. Many of these "Bulldog" programs are primarily volunteer driven.

Common characteristics of large sustainable alumni-driven programs. See Appendix for chart of local Bulldogs programs.

❑ **Location is far from the university.** Local alumni introduce the employers, students, employment agencies, and university career services to each other. (In a city near the university, employers and the university easily find each other – and communicate directly.)

❑ **Located in a mid-size city** where alumni are business leaders who feel that the city by itself is not attracting sufficient talent, or diverse enough talent. Most successful Bulldog programs are in cities with populations of 300,000 to 800,000 and metro populations of 1 million to 3.5 million supporting 20 – 50 internships each summer. To entice students to accept an internship for the summer, these programs offer free housing, strong community programming, mentoring, and group activities. In contrast, large cities are sufficiently attractive to students that there is not a need for these extra incentives to attract applicants for internships.

❑ **Presence of an active regional alumni association.** All currently successful Bulldogs Across America programs have been supported by Clubs in an area with about 500 to 1500 alumni within a relatively compact area providing enough volunteers and donors to run the program.

❑ **Houses the interns together (or in close proximity)** and for free. Providing housing may mean participating employers incur an additional cost or the organizers have to secure donations from other alumni (especially for NGO internships). Most Bulldog programs arrange housing for interns economically at a local university though some provide homestays. The residential component creates a community for the students who might be concerned that they would not have enjoyable leisure time experiences, or meet interesting people.

❑ **Alumni mentor the students**, and sometimes engage alumni families to share leisure activities with the students.

❑ **Alumni arrange for special group activities** for the students.

Brand your internship program. Your university name recognition and identity will make it easier to publicize to students, easier to recruit employers, easier to generate internships, easier to start up a similar program in a new city, and easier to recruit alumni support. Use a similar name for many of your student-internship programs. Pick a name that will rally alumni and that even non-alumni will identify with the school, such as a school mascot or color.

Yale "Bulldogs". Two of the largest internship programs at Yale use the name "bulldogs", which is the name of the Yale mascot. Internship applications are facilitated by Yale's Office of Career Services (OCS), though some of the actual internship programs are administered by local alumni through AYA Regional Associations (e.g. Community Service Fellowships and Bulldogs Across America).

❑ Bulldogs Across America is really seven similar, independent programs run by local alumni in seven different cities across the United States: *http://ocs.yale.edu/content/domestic-internships-program-alumni-sponsored-housing-mentoring-and-events* .

❑ International Bulldogs is a broad program administered through OCS, as part of Yale's globalization initiatives.

Partner with other universities. Sometimes it is necessary for several universities to combine resources for a sustainable summer student internship program which may require re-branding. Bulldogs in the Rockies (Denver, CO) has evolved to serve six universities and is now co-branded as Bulldogs in the Rockies/CLIMB or just C.L.I.M.B. (Colorado Leaders, Interns, Mentors in Business: *http:// www.climbtherockies.org*). Bulldogs on the Cuyahoga (Cleveland, OH) includes eight universities under the new name of Summer on the Cuyahoga (*http://www.summeronthecuyahoga.com*). OCS no longer does intake for this program, but the local Yale Club is still deeply involved.

13.3 | Regional Associations Abroad key factors for success

Regional associations abroad are distant from the alma mater in both space and culture. Kilometers alone pose significant challenges. Perhaps foremost is "out of sight, out of mind" from the perspective of both far-flung alumni and their university's administrators. Mutual invisibility is reinforced by the cost of travel in both time and money. In addition, distance from campus often implies few and dispersed alumni, making local self-organization difficult and significant assistance from the university neither cheap nor easy.

Distance in culture imposes additional pressures: legal, lingual, social, and cultural. Alumni organization structures need to fit the local legal requirements. Alumni may have returned to their home country or they may be ex-pats based in a city for just two or three years. The interests and purpose of these two different groups of alumni for engaging with the university may not align. And alumni abroad may find it harder to find each other, though they may be even more interested in connecting because of their shared experience. All of these considerations may require the university to find different ways to provide support.

These key factors motivate the following suggestions, not just for local volunteer leaders on-the-ground, but also the university support for them.

Local leadership. Strong local leadership is essential for the success of an international club. Strong leaders might form a regional association on their own. If the region or area or country is important to the institution, the University can think about recruiting one or more local alumni with leadership capacity, and asking them to establish a club. In either case, the University must be prepared to offer support in the way of alumni lists or communicating with regional alumni on behalf of the regional association, basic resources, visits from faculty or the alumni relations office, and guidance. It's lonely "out there." The University can help to make it less so.

Alumni "density." A successful association needs a critical mass. There is no special, exact formula for this. A truly dynamic leader can bring people together, while the lack of a leader can keep a crowd from becoming a club. Still, alumni density might determine your priorities in developing clubs, and where you aim your resources. A city or region with a lot of alumni is more likely to have a (potential) leader, and more likely to build ongoing momentum, than one where alumni are few and far between.

Key items for support from the university.

- ❏ **A good, up-to-date alumni list** and support for list maintenance. *Even if privacy laws prohibit sharing the list itself with a regional association, the university needs to be able to process alumni information that the regional association provides. For example, an alumnus or alumna might inform the local chapter that he or she has moved into the region (or will be moving out of it), without telling the university. Even if privacy laws prohibit sharing the list, the university has to work with the local chapters to find ways to contact and welcome alumni who have just moved into the region.* Provide advice and policies on how to deal with names on the list (opt-in, opt-out on e-mailings, what not to do with the names)

- ❏ **Internet or website support.** *Habemus website, ergo sumus.* This might include advice on Facebook or LinkedIn for groups. Setting up a webpage or website takes too much time and energy when each group has to explore the matter on its own.

- ❏ **Some basic training in resources and requirements.** Spend an hour or two walking the local leader through available resources.

Introduce new leaders to more experienced leaders and to other local leaders. Do *not* assume that just because two of your volunteers are in the same foreign country (or city) they will know each other. Introduce them.

For example, in the Netherlands, the Yale Admissions Office wanted local Yale alumni to interview Dutch high school students applying for admission to Yale. The Admissions Office even had a Yale alumni volunteer in the Netherlands willing to organize the interviews. However, the Admissions Office never linked that volunteer with the regional association leaders. They met by chance – and all worked out well. But do not rely on serendipity.

Remember. A good candidate for leading a regional alumni association may have leadership experience, but not necessarily with alumni. While running a volunteer organization can be quite different from running a formal organization with hierarchies and reporting lines, leadership skills may be relevant.

❏ **Ties to the "mothership."** An organization built around a far-off university is buoyed by frequent contact. Pay particular attention to travel schedules, and arrange events around travelling faculty or university representatives if possible, and local alumni. It takes a little bit of work, but is greatly appreciated by the club, and strengthens the ties tremendously.

Alumni umbrella groups. If there are not enough alumni in one area to create a robust association, consider looking into "like-minded" groups and forming an umbrella group that might include a few different universities. Consider peers based on rankings, country of origin, size, or school focus (e.g. business school alumni, computer science majors, etc.) A regional association might have one or two "exclusive" events and a few "shared" events to provide a fuller calendar. The good experience of the Ivy Circle in the Netherlands is an example, as are the "Oxbridge" clubs and a number of Ivy+ organizations. Many overseas U.S. university alumni associations get together with associations from other universities on a regular, if informal, basis to create a critical mass for events.

Remember. A vital local alumni organization can help you recruit students, raise the university's profile, and build bonds in numerous ways.

See also 16.1 Day of Service Abroad

For planning a regional conference, see 14.2 Convocations, Conferences, and Colloquia involving alumni volunteers.

Chapter 14

Graduate and Professional Schools (Convocations and Colloquia)

For the purposes of the information presented here, "graduate and professional schools" refer to those educational institutions that usually require the student to first get a degree from a 4 year college or university program. Graduate and professional schools usually confer a Masters or Doctorate degree and in the U.S. it would include a law degree.

The undergraduate education in many countries is shorter or more focused than in the U.S. Consequently, educational institutions outside the U.S. may experience some of the same difficulties organizing alumni, which are evident at many U.S. graduate and professional schools.

Also, when most young people serve in the military before university, the undergraduate student experience is more like the graduate student experience in the U.S. Many of the bonds of friendship that in the U.S. are formed among college students in their late teens are instead formed among the young members of a military unit.

14.1 | Graduate School Alumni Organizations constraints and opportunities

Graduate and Professional Schools often have a small class size and a specialized curriculum that can affect the cohesiveness of the alumni population and the best opportunities for engagement. Programing for alumni may range from class reunions to school-wide convocations, from receptions at industry events to industry-specific mentoring, from university speakers at venues around the country (or world) to alumni-run regional gatherings.

This range of activities may be limited due to institutional constraints or resources. The types of programs that attract alumni may reflect a smaller set of fellow students who are friends or a lessened feeling of connectedness to the school. Nonetheless, there are opportunities to connect and build community.

On-campus opportunities for engagement. Despite fewer numbers the increased commonality of career goals and career value of networking may help make get-togethers work.

❏ **Larger professional schools** have enough students graduating each year to hold quinquennial (every 5 years) reunions for each cohort. This may vary from university to university, but may include law schools, business schools, or med schools with a set number of years of education so that the students that begin together also graduate together.

❏ **Smaller graduate or professional schools** may hold a school-wide homecoming or alumni weekend every year – sometimes with special events for quinquennial "reunion" cohorts. At Yale, the law school, the divinity school, and the forestry school hold these combined type of events.

❏ **Smaller-yet schools** might hold a homecoming or school-wide reunion only once every several years. At Yale, the Drama School and the School of Public Health follow this model. There might be special reunions for particular classes (such as the 25th or 50th reunion) – depending upon class interest. The Yale Graduate School of Arts & Sciences holds a colloquium every year, but focused on a different department – and attracting a different set of alumni.

Off-campus opportunities. The Yale Drama School sponsors receptions at industry conventions such as the United States Institute for Theatre Technology (USITT) which serves design, production, and technology professionals in the performing arts and entertainment industry. In addition, because many of the graduates of the Drama School work in either New York or Hollywood, the Drama School organizes two parties each year – one in New York in December and one on the West Coast in the Los Angeles area at another time such as March.

Alumni of the Indian Institutes of Technology have found an interesting way of addressing low numbers and scattered alumni. They have formed an organization that organizes a Pan-IIT convocation every year. One year it will be located in a city in the U.S. – the next year it will be in a city in India: see *http://iit.org/conferences/*. See also *http://www.iitalumnicanada.com/page-1710539* for Pan-IIT alumni in Canada.

14.2 | Convocations, Conferences, and Colloquia involving alumni volunteers

Holding events at university. *Convocations, conferences, and colloquia are often planned, organized, and produced at university – and for the most part by the event planners at and employees of university.* This is true even if alumni are invited.

However, **to the extent that the event is intended to promote a sense of community among alumni and students it is important to involve them** (and not just university academics and administrators). This means more than inviting relevant alumni and/or students. It means including them in planning, organizing and producing the event. This is true even if university-based administrators and academics are an important part of the program.

In these respects, convocations, conferences, and colloquia are like reunions.

❑ The Assembly of the Association of Yale Alumni brings 500 alumni volunteer leaders to Yale for several days every autumn. While most of the back-end is accomplished by AYA professionals, much of the planning, including choice of topics, venues, and speakers, involves significant input from the Yale alumni volunteer leaders who comprise the AYA Board of Governors.

❑ The Yale Graduate School as well as Yale's individual Professional Schools each hold conferences and colloquia back at Yale which involve input from alumni.

❑ YaleGALE @Yale is based on programming developed by volunteers, with much of the work performed by volunteers. At the same time coordination by AYA professional staff, who are on location, is essential. In addition the event is enhanced because

Yale administrators and alumni relations professionals are able to appear at the event.

Taking the "show" on the road. Often a university representative, fundraiser, top administrator (or group of administrators) will present essentially the same program in different locations around the country or around the world. This is true even if all the speakers come from campus. Reasons for such outreach vary: (a) alumni may have difficulty scheduling travel back to university and (b) a "destination" event may attract a different set of alumni.

A university produced event may also be held off campus when closer to the locus of key speakers.

Although local alumni and their regional association may not be instrumental in planning or producing the event, involving them in publicizing and promoting the event may be a key to generating attendance. Websites, emails, other social media, and word-of-mouth are important to building an audience for the event.

Supporting regional volunteer-run events. Conferences and colloquia may be initiated by one or more alumni volunteers who live far from campus. They may come up with the idea for an event. They may be willing and able to do much of the planning, organizing and producing for the event – but sometimes only if the event is located near where they live. Examples for Yale alumni include:

- Social enterprise conference in New York City produced by the Yale Alumni Nonprofit Alliance (YANA) a shared interest group: *http://yalenonprofitalliance.org/events/spring-2014-event/*
- Healthcare conference in Oregon produced in conjunction with the Yale Club of Oregon and Southwest Washington: *http://yaleclubor.org/healthcare/agenda/*

Of course, some regional conferences involve both volunteer-run events produced by a regional association and events produced by the university. See for example the city-wide celebration of the founding of St. Louis, in which both Yale University and local Yale Club participated: *http://www.aya.yale.edu/sites/default/files/images/clubs/Case%20Study%20Yale%20Club%20of%20St.%20Louis%20PDF.pdf* .

Key tasks for local volunteer(s) include

❑ **Decide on and secure a keynote speaker early.** Then build the event around him or her. A well-chosen keynote speaker will draw an audience for the event.

❑ **Determine costs early – especially fixed costs.** This allows you to price the event properly and establish break-even attendance.

❑ **Enroll help from both the regional alumni association and the alumni relations team on campus.** Strong support from the university-based professional staff can be priceless – even if the locals provide "boots on the ground". Be sure to acknowledge alumni association staff during the event (and afterwards).

❑ **Enlist motivated local partner(s) and/or sponsor(s)** (when appropriate). Useful ongoing collaboration can result.

❑ **Consider securing continuing education credits**, if the event is geared towards professionals.

❑ **Create a marketing calendar.** This will keep you on track. Involve your local partner(s) and sponsor(s). Consider how best to use social media to market the event.

University-based alumni relations professionals may need to help inspire and empower the local alumni volunteer leader(s). Nonetheless, the volunteer(s) needs to be motivated, organized, and skilled in forming and leading a team.

Some things to keep in mind.

❑ **The richest conference experience often occurs outside the meeting rooms** – at lunch, breaks, random encounters. Build in plenty of opportunities to create these experiences.

❑ **Refreshments are vital!** Provide sufficient snacks and drinks to keep people fueled and energized.

❑ **The payoff from a conference often comes from the post-event follow up.** Make it easy for attendees to find each other afterwards. Provide contact info where possible (and legal). You may need to secure permission.

For a checklist to help plan a local conference or gala (or indeed any local event) see page 4 of the online toolkit provided by the Yale Alumni Nonprofit Alliance: *http://yalenonprofitalliance.org/wp-content/uploads/2014/04/YANA-Nonprofit-Career-Toolkit-April-2014.pdf* .

For materials on planning a graduate or professional school reunion or homecoming:
See 12.1 and 12.2 Reunions – part 1 and part 2

Chapter 15

Shared Interest Groups and Affinity Groups

All affinity groups are different. All have characteristics in common. Much of what YaleGALE has to share concerning affinity and shared interest groups is in Part II (organizing volunteer communities). Despite differences, all SIGs are organized in similar ways. Volunteers are recruited in similar ways. Leadership is cultivated (and leaders are mentored) in similar ways. The words "Thank you" remain magical – and the currency of the realm.

On-campus gatherings and convocations, programs and events, all require similar types of planning efforts described in Chapters 12, 13, and 14. **Thematic conferences are covered in detail in Chapter 14.2.**

Consequently, although some particular affinity groups at Yale have been described in Part I, organizational and operational questions are addressed elsewhere.

For material about organizing affinity groups see:

❏ See 8.1 Affinity Groups

❏ See 8.2 Organizing Alumni by Interests and Passions

❏ See 8.3 Creating a Community around Travel

❏ See 8.4 Building Alumni Community through Athletics

❏ See also 7.3 Leadership and Governance

❏ See also two online Case Studies of YaleWomen: www.yalegale.org/resources/wp-content/uploads/2014/07/YaleWomen_starting_chapters.pdf and www.yalegale.org/resources/wp-content/uploads/2013/01/YaleWomen-Case-Study-011413.pdf

THE YaleGALE Guide

For materials on programming for a regional SIG chapter see the materials on Clubs and Regional Associations
- 13.1 Programs to Sustain Alumni Engagement
  - 13.1.1 Engaging Alumni of Different Ages
  - 13.1.2 List of sample regional association activities
- 13.2 Student Internships, Mentoring, and alumni participation
  - 13.2.1 Creating a "Bulldogs" Intern Program
  - Appendix 1 Bulldogs Across America Data
- 13.3 Regional Associations Abroad
- 16.1 Day of Service Abroad

For materials on planning an affinity group reunion
- 12.1 and 12.2 Reunions – part 1 and part 2

For more on producing a conference
- 14.2 Convovations, Conferences, Colloquia involving alumni volunteers

Chapter 16

Service Programs and Initiatives

Yale has a long tradition of "service" as a university cultural value. This has been manifest in organized student volunteer activities such as providing tutoring to inner city youth. Many alumni regional associations have had service projects and activities for many decades. The new thrust of alumni programming at AYA which began in 2007-2008 has been to organize such activities on a national (or international) basis and make them available for all alumni to participate.

An important point is that in addition to personal satisfaction by volunteering in service projects, this "giving of oneself" for a worthy cause is a way to participate in a social alumni event. Importantly from an organizational consideration for a national or regional alumni organization, service projects are one more piece in the repertoire of the planning committee and one that brings in many alumni who would not otherwise be involved with the university. In addition, a service project, as a participatory event, allows many who might not feel comfortable with each other in a more overtly "social" situation to bond in service and socially.

In some senses, these initiatives are like shared interest groups, where the shared interest is performing a certain type of volunteer service or charitable deed.

Three of these initiatives (Yale Alumni Service Corps, YASA and YaleGALE, described in Part I) combine a passion for service with a passion for travel – though each focuses on a different type of volunteer service. More such initiatives are contemplated. A key is to find a type of service that can be performed in conjunction with an appropriate travel itinerary. (See Chapter 8.3)

Perhaps the most wide-spread alumni service activity, the Yale

Day of Service (also described in Part I), serves not only as a self-contained program with local efforts coordinated by regional, national, and international volunteers, but also as an entry point for regional associations or local SIG chapters to initiate service projects of their own. Some service programs that started as Day of Service projects become repeatable, expandable, and self-sustaining – and rallying points for local volunteer efforts of regional associations or shared interest groups.

16.1 | Day of Service Abroad

Volunteering and performing service may not resonate in a university's culture, especially when performed in its home-country. *But, out-of-country service can still be a powerful organizing force.*

Volunteering for many types of NGOs is endemic in America. It's been prevalent since the 1700s even before it was an independent country. It was remarked upon to great effect in the 1800s by Alexis de Tocqueville as a unique characteristic of American culture. This is not the case everywhere.

If your university is located in a country with a well-developed social safety net and high taxes designed to pay for it, alumni may feel that social services and social justice are the government's duty. It may be hard to generate enthusiasm for volunteering for an in-country service project. Nonetheless, people may strongly support projects such as Doctors Without Borders (*Médecins Sans Frontières*) which provide such services to underserved communities in countries or regions where the safety net is not intact or so well developed. They may even choose to participate in a program in an underserved community in another country.

This emotional reservoir to help can be tapped by out-of-country regional alumni associations (or chapters) organizing service projects for alumni living abroad in many countries. *A Day of Service project may be a simple and effective opening for engaging alumni to bring their energy to the university in a new way.*

The benefits of organizing a Day of Service in out-of-country alumni chapters.

❏ It provides networking (and bonding) opportunities among alumni.

❏ It provides unique opportunities to meet, network, and bond with service-minded non-alumni locals. Because this is neither a business nor strictly social setting, alumni can make important local contacts to which they would not otherwise have access. Participating in a service project may break down social and networking barriers to outsiders and foreigners.

❏ It provides an opportunity to enhance the brand of the school (and hence its alumni) to both the served populace as well as non-alumni volunteers involved in the service project. It is a way to develop goodwill towards the university, regardless of political differences.

❏ It helps demonstrate to the local community – by voluntarily giving back – that university alumni (often foreign nationals) value their opportunity to work in that community.

❏ For an international chapter in a country where volunteering is highly valued (such as a chapter in the US), it helps demonstrate an adoption of some important local cultural moral values.

❏ Of course, if volunteering is a key cultural value at the university, then it becomes an important organizing principle for any out-of-country regional chapter. As discussed elsewhere, a Day of Service project is often an easy way to begin planning these type of events and engaging these cultural values.

Cultural attitudes in the host community may make organizing easier.

❏ In a country where not-for-profits or NGOs are involved in service projects, they often welcome participation by other groups (as a group) in their projects. This is certainly true in the US, and is one of the key ways that Yale Clubs plan their Day of Service events. (See below.)

❏ In a country where not-for-profits or NGOs are prevalent, they often partner with other organizations on small projects that further their mission.

❏ In a country where voluntary service is a cultural norm, government entities such as parks, schools, and libraries, also offer volunteering and partnering opportunities.

❏ Many Yale Clubs around the world are always looking for Day of Service volunteers, and welcome anyone who is willing to participate.

Much about organizing a Day of Service program is the same wherever you are. It still takes dedicated local volunteer leaders (see Chapter 16.2 below). However, university encouragement and recruitment can be key to making the program work. It may be helpful for recruiting alumni volunteers to make local out-of-country efforts part of a university sponsored (and branded) international program – where the university is providing online organizing tools and social media support (see Chapter 11.3 above).

An alumni regional association abroad may have fewer members than one back home, making organizing any event harder. However, in some circumstances cultural attitudes may be leveraged to make organizing a Day of Service abroad a good option.

16.2 | Planning a local Day of Service

Organizing an annual Day of Service where alumni can make a difference in their local communities brings alumni together and refreshes their ties with the university. The event and ensuing success stories promote a virtuous cycle of community engagement, alumni pride, and visibility for the university: *www.yaledayofservice.org*. (Helpful organizing tips can be found at the Yale Day of Service website: *http://yaledayofservice.org/organizers-toolbox*.)

Local volunteer leadership is key. You need a volunteer leader dedicated to the outreach efforts and passionate about the idea. The leader must support individual, local service project pioneers with materials, guidelines, encouragement and recognition. Broadcasting success stories from these pioneer projects to all alumni will start a snowball effect, encouraging other alumni service entrepreneurs to step forward to organize projects.

Maintaining the energy requires tenacious attention to several tasks.

❑ **Communicate, communicate, communicate.** Tell success stories about beneficiaries of your service projects, using photos and their words. Use email, letters, websites and social media to keep the messages alive.

❑ **Energetically recognize alumni** who have led or participated as volunteers in the projects with personal thank you notes and publication of their quotes and photos.

❑ **Continuously improve your support materials** and processes including service project registration tools, waiver forms, promotional materials, media templates, thank you letter templates, planning checklists for the organizers and event preparation checklists for the project coordinators and volunteers.

How do you find and develop local service projects? It is essential to create a partnership with a local service organization such as a school, association, NGO or other experienced charitable organization. The partner can be helpful where the density of alumni is low and the lack of critical mass seems to be an obstacle for the local alumni entrepreneur.

❑ **Service partners provide help** with additional service ideas and volunteers to reinforce your alumni volunteers.

❑ **Hold regular planning sessions** with the partner to create a simple program plan and follow up on the planning tasks.

❑ **FOCUS on 1 or 2 great service ideas** that will be successful and rewarding for all.

How do you recruit volunteers for a Day of Service? You need three types of volunteers: a leading pioneer who will bring the idea to life in a specific region or country; two or more people who are willing to serve on the core planning team; and volunteers for the actual day who will serve as project leaders and/or volunteers working on the project.

❏ **Attract interest through success stories** and recognition of alumni in other regions who have stepped forward. Share the fun! People like to join successful, productive, humane projects.

❏ **Make it easy to participate** through a clear statement of what is expected in terms of time and effort, simple sign-up sites and a variety of support materials and guidelines.

❏ **Have a contingency plan** with local service partner(s) to ensure a back-up source of volunteers.

❏ **Thank volunteers** who commit early to serve and follow up with them to make sure they show up.

❏ **Make all projects visible** to all alumni worldwide so that they can participate in another region during a trip.

How much extra cost will be involved? If the university chooses to devote resources to a professional to manage the Day of Service program, the expense is spread across many sites that encompass the whole international effort. Importantly, the regional associations, the local projects and any other sponsors do not contribute to underwriting that cost. However, local projects might have their own expenses for printed materials, t-shirts/hats, and a post-event social gathering amongst participating alumni. One Day of Service in Switzerland cost the local alumni club about 100 Euros for these local ancillary costs.

How do you reinforce the team? Make the activity fun and rewarding in itself. In addition, there is a certain gratifying feeling that comes from making a difference in the lives of other people in your community.

❏ **For the core team.** Arrange a couple of after-work meetings in a nice cafe to check on progress and socialize. Lasting relationships between alumni are built through this teamwork that focuses on a common goal. Weekend skype sessions combining personal catch-up and task follow-up have also worked well.

❏ **For service project volunteers.** For encouragement, provide regular communication about what will be expected of them, clear logistics information, and good project leadership.

❑ **For all.** Give a heartfelt "thank you" to each volunteer and service partner. Recognize projects and teams in university communications.

See 8.3 Creating a Community around Travel.
See 11.4 Planning Multiple-Location Events using social media

The YaleGALE Guide

 PART IV

FUNDRAISING

Volunteers can have an important role in fundraising efforts. Certainly, in the past 50 years, fundraising techniques have progressed. There are advanced degree programs in the field so professionals and consultants abound. Nonetheless, when properly deployed, volunteers can augment fundraising efforts. Of course volunteers who help raise funds must be recruited, engaged, retained, and motivated – and the principles and examples from Part II (on organizing volunteer communities) apply. Some organizations, such as the Yale Alumni Fund, rely upon volunteers to lead, train, and organize other volunteers as discussed in Part II. This chapter will focus on the special issues related to using volunteers to seek and request donations to an organization or cause.

An organization that uses volunteers for fundraising may hold special events for them. For example, the Yale Alumni Fund holds bi-annual convocations for volunteer leaders (during a capital campaign, the convocation may be held every year). Such convocations or assemblies have organizational characteristics similar in some respects to homecomings and reunions, see for example Chapter 12 in this Part III.

For many universities and other educational institutions around the world, an increased interest in alumni relations is due to an increased interest in getting alumni to donate money. At many educational institutions, the alumni relations department is also in charge of fundraising (and may be tasked with communications and public relations as well). At Yale, alumni relations and development are separate departments with distinct responsibilities that report to the same vice president. But we recognize that wearing several hats (such as friend-raising and fundraising) may affect department priorities and policies. Nonetheless, to the extent that the institution uses volunteer help, this section should be of use.

THE YaleGALE Guide

Chapter 17

Development 101

Before considering how best to use volunteers to help raise money, it is best to touch on some of the underlying principles of fundraising today. These concepts are by no means exhaustive or the only ways to raise funds. However, when volunteers are involved as fundraisers they either have to learn these basics on their own – or someone has to teach them. A quick review of these fundamentals also suggests some of the most productive ways to deploy volunteers.

17.1 | The Fundraising Cycle and Donor Motivation

Basic concepts in Development and Fundraising

"Development" is the thoughtful process of building relationships that advance an institution's mission over time, including setting goals to raise funds to accomplish that mission. When relationships are developed with care, donors make gifts that truly help the cause rather than offering gifts that divert from the mission.

"Fundraising" is the process of asking for and obtaining funds to advance a cause.

Charitable giving has existed as long as people have interacted in their communities, and has enabled communities to create NGOs, hospitals, schools and universities, and encourage arts, research, and networking

The Five Steps in the Fundraising Cycle. In the United States, fundraising and development are well-studied, almost-scientific fields. Research has documented best practices for the American culture that result in generous support from donors. Most importantly, successful

fundraising is all about relationships and the donor's desire to have impact. In simplified terms, the five basic steps are:
- ❏ **Identification.** Find prospective donors ("prospects").
- ❏ **Interest.** Determine whether the prospect has any link to your cause (being an alumnus is a start but is not sufficient).
- ❏ **Involvement.** This is the longest stage: Cultivate the prospect and engage them in the interests of the institution.
- ❏ **Solicitation.** Ask for a specific gift – based on the interests of the donor and the need of the institution.
- ❏ **Stewardship.** Thank the donor in every possible way – with reports, events, and concrete ways so they may see the results of their gift.

The five steps run in a continuous cycle: a gift that is properly stewarded leads to the process of identifying a further gift opportunity from the donor to the institution, and to the deepening of the donor's relationship to the cause, and to the advancement of the cause.

Motivations for Giving. In the U.S. there is a "culture of giving" that recognizes a wide variety of motivations for donating. While children learn from an early age that "giving back" and helping others is expected as a member of any community, it is also important to recognize that people give for different reasons and might give to difference institutions for different reasons. When soliciting a donation of treasure or time or talent, it helps to understand the motivation of the donor so that you have the right approach and can have a meaningful discussion.

There are some theories that consider the motivations for giving to be based on a progression or hierarchy of giving in which a selfless, altruistic, and anonymous gift is considered the highest level of giving. Practically and realistically speaking, understanding and respecting the breadth of motivations is far more important. The primary motivations for giving can be categorized as:

❏ **Rewards and Recognition.** A donor wants to be publicly acknowledged whether to further his/her community status, to feel self-gratification as a generous person, or to leave a recognized legacy for posterity. A reward might range from a small gift to a publicly presented certificate to engraving a donors name on the wall of a building.

❑ **Access to fascinating people and fun events.** Donors of funds or of time are often invited to special events, perhaps providing access to high-profile people from within the institution such as the President or Vice-Chancellor or a related person such as a movie star. While your highest level donors may enjoy these benefits, someone interested primarily in these aspects is not likely to be your biggest giver.

❑ **Strong belief in the cause or the people who direct it.** People give to an entity that they feel has a worthwhile mission that they want to support and that is successful in realizing that mission. Closely related, donors will give because they believe in the leadership of the organization. This may be because a leader is a personal friend, a professional colleague, or an effective trusted manager. In order to gather this type of support, the cause, the methodology and the effectiveness of the organization must be clearly expressed and communicated to the potential donor.

❑ **Desire to make a difference in their community and in the world.** In the words of the American Revolutionary war hero Nathan Hale, "I wish to be useful." Being useful and making a difference in your community or another community has a positive chemical effect on the human body for everyone. It is human instinct although many people do not realize it until they actually start giving back. This type of motivation is usually a selfless motivation as people are giving to help others, not to help themselves and not for recognition. Often, the giver may wish to remain anonymous while effecting change.

❑ **Urge to give back to society.** A potential donor of time, talent or treasure may have a broad motive to give back. Similarly, the donor may have a personal history with the organization that compels giving as a means of both thanking the organization for the opportunities given the donor and ensuring that these opportunities are available for others. Such donors would be looking to have the greatest impact possible for the resources contributed. The donor might be grateful for having a certain lifestyle that has luxury and enough to give to others. Or the donor might feel that giving back to society is something that any and all individuals should be doing. As the person is looking for a worthy cause, there is an excellent opportunity to work with the prospective donor on behalf of your organization.

❏ **Sense of Belonging.** A university or other organization is based on a community whether of students and faculty or volunteers or shared goals. With respect to universities, see below in the section Preparing a Student for a Lifetime of Giving.

❏ **May give for tax benefits, but this is not the sole motivator.** In the U.S. and some other places, giving money directly or spending money on behalf of a charitable organization can provide a tax benefit. This motivation can spur people to give a larger gift or give a gift at a particular time however it will not be a sole motivator nor will it make your organization specifically attractive as this benefit applies to all charities in the U.S.

Every Gift Matters. Gifts at all levels make a difference. Large capital gifts may have transformational impact. Annual giving at more modest levels promotes participation and demonstrates the breadth of philanthropic support by members of a community. Small gifts may lead to large ones, when the donors are thoughtfully stewarded!

17.2 | The Intimate Face of Fundraising

Fundraising has many facets from mass market campaigns that raise hundreds of millions of dollars, to solicitations of mere handfuls of donors that raise as much. Which approach, or mix of approaches, is best depends upon the donor base – and how the fundraising campaign is linked to other organization goals. In many campaigns, a variation of the "Pareto principle" applies: that 80% of the donations are made by 20% of the donors. Some campaigns are even more skewed, with perhaps 90% to 95% of the contributions given by only 5% to 10% of the contributors. In such campaigns, it becomes important to maximize the contributions of the relative few. Fundraising becomes more intimate, and the interactions between the person who solicits a gift (the gift "solicitor") and the prospective donor become paramount. **Solicitor-based fundraising is a very delicate and sensitive art.** *It is best done in person and face-to-face.* Next best is over the telephone. The more impersonal the ask, the less likely it is to be effective, and the less likely to yield optimal gifts. Getting to know the donor and developing a relationship typically generates the big gifts. Matching a donor's passion with the need of the institution is crucial, but the personal relationship is key. The art of "the ask" is about listening carefully to a donor's words and demeanor and responding thoughtfully and with nuance to the donor's particular history, situation, and desires.

Donating is about supporting a community – and the people within it – with which the donor identifies. This is why it is essential for fundraisers to build connections with the donor, and between the donor and the community for which "the ask" is made. One of these connections is the solicitation itself. There is no substitute for being part of a real-world in-flesh community. However, online communities can keep connections alive when people are distant, or introduce people to a group that they embrace in real life. This is especially true for younger generations, where maintaining an active and vibrant virtual community using social media can be essential to fundraising – even when the ask is not made online.

Fundraising can lose polish and effectiveness when applied on a mass scale with social media. An impersonal ask is the easiest to ignore. People may "unfollow" an online community that is used only to ask for gifts. (The same holds true of all communications – whether snail-mail or email – if viewed by the recipient as solely "marketing" or "soliciting".) For many organizations, utilizing social media primarily as a community builder is likely to attract more followers/friends. These can be approached for raising funds on a more individual and personal basis.

Develop a database of prospective donors and their contact information. This is essential for all fundraising – whether or not solicitor-based. *Social media and online communities may be a key component of the database gathering effort.*

Stay connected to alumni who will give during the course of their lives. Establish a meaningful lifetime relationship driven by customer service, tailored programs built on market data, and career services.

- **The Napa Group**, *www.napagroup.com*, Trends and Best Practices in Alumni Associations.

    ▶ Use market information and data to segment programs and create value-centric relationships with alumni; shift toward lifetime relationships through a "lifecycle model of programs and services."

    ▶ Alumni seek meaningful relationships with their universities; alumni relations become 'portals' for programming and communications and an 'enabler' of services.

- **Engagealumni.com**, *http://engagealumni.com/tag/alumni-relations-best-practices/* – Building Alumni Affinity through Great Customer Service – user friendly websites, easy access to live support, seamless logistics at events, knowing what alumni expect.

- **Team Works Media**, *http://www.teamworksmedia.com/blog/university-engagement-5-new-ways-to-think-alumni/* – No one size fits all – "The emotional engagement button is different between (and often within) generations and if you don't parse your message accordingly you'll miss the mark on triggering a response."

- **Jewish Philanthrophy**, *http://ejewishphilanthropy.com/keep-alumni-engaged-by-offering-career-services/* – "At the core of every successful alumni program ... is an ability to capture and reflect back what the members want. One of the best ways to engage alumni is by offering them resources and support in making decisions about their career."

- **CASE**, *www.case.org*, Multiple articles in areas of Outreach and Engagement, Constituencies, Alumni Generations, and Marketing & Market Research.

17.3 | Capital Campaigns
high impact philanthropy

Differences between a capital campaign and an annual campaign. Capital campaigns were originally multi-year efforts to raise funds for specific physical capital improvement projects such as a building. The term has come to mean any multi-year fundraising effort for specific well-defined goals. In contrast, an annual campaign raises funds for current (and typically unrestricted) operating expenses. Both capital and annual campaigns involve specific accounting practices.

The largest "cornerstone" gifts to capital campaigns often – but by no means always – are the result of personal relationships nurtured over time and on trust and motivated by shared priorities.

In capital campaigns, donors are asked to give from both their assets and their income. They are asked for "stretch" gifts, not easy or ordinary ones. Gifts are often pledges paid over multiple years (sometimes even beyond the life of the campaign). For more on large capital or "stretch" gifts see: *http://philanthropynewsdigest.org/news/so-called-stretch-gifts-growing-in-popularity* . Various methodologies can be used for determining an individual's giving capacity and inclination. See: *http://www.apragny.org/calendar/events_0708/docs/071106_apravs_bw3.pdf* . Good prospect research (which accurately assesses prospects' capacity, inclination, and priority interests) can make or break a capital campaign.

The types of capital campaigns

❑ **Comprehensive campaigns.** More typical of universities and colleges, all types of giving count in the totals, including annual giving, planned giving, as well as gifts for facilities, current use programs, and endowment. They usually last 5 – 7 years (or longer) with a 2 – 3 year "quiet phase," followed by a public phase. They are often linked to institutional strategic plans and address important priorities that have the potential to advance the institution significantly.

❑ **Single-priority campaigns.** More typical of independent or boarding schools and cultural institutions, these efforts usually focus on endowment OR facilities OR financial aid, etc. They usually last 2 – 5 years, and may rely on a few key donors and not include a highly-public phase.

The stages of a capital campaign. A capital campaign used to be a once-in-a-lifetime event, but many development efforts now run in a continuous cycle. There is a planning stage, a quiet fundraising stage, a public fundraising stage, and a quiescent time before the next capital campaign begins.

The planning phase is essential to a successful campaign. It occurs before the campaign is even launched.

- ❑ **Commission a Feasibility Study**, to determine (a) inclination and capacity of identified constituency to give to the institution and (b) the appropriate monetary goal considering results of study.

- ❑ **Recruit and train a professional staff** with the expertise needed to reach goal(s). Equip them with high-quality in-depth prospect research and an accurate, flexible, and responsive database.

- ❑ **Determine campaign priorities.** Make sure these are linked to the institution's mission and resonate with the constituency.

- ❑ **Solidify campaign leadership.** Senior staff should commit to stay in their positions until end of campaign; key volunteer leadership should be identified and recruited.

For a discussion of the campaign stages written as a workbook, see *http://www.grassrootsfundraising.org/wp-content/uploads/2011/08/Conquer-Capital-Campaigns-Wkbk.pdf* . See also: *www.capitalcampaigns.com* .

- ❑ 25 years ago, typically 80% of the money was contributed by 20% of the donors; today it is closer to 95% contriburted by 5%.

- ❑ A campaign is typically not made public until 35% – 50% of the goal has been achieved.

- ❑ The amount contributed by the Board depends on the size and constituency of the Board and the Campaign goals; it can range from 10% – 50%.

Some hints to running a successful campaign: focus on the critical few who can make large leadership commitments, but provide opportunities for the faithful rank and file to play a role; frame your need in terms of community benefits, train volunteers to close gifts, and have the courage to stand behind a dollar goal and a deadline. *https:// www.guidestar.org/Articles.aspx?path=/rxa/news/articles/2012/five-capital-campaign-secrets.aspx* .

Engaging the volunteers and non-professionals. Most successful campaigns actively involve the organization's CEO and governing Board – even when they are volunteers. For some organizations a key function of such boards is fundraising. Some ways to get their enthusiastic buy-in: deal directly with their distaste for fundraising, explain that it is not about the money (it's about changing lives), empower them to seek friends not donors, focus on the important jobs not involving "the ask" such as creating new friends, involving current ones, and thanking donors: *http://www.gailperry.com/board-training/get-your-board-members-fired-up-and-in-action-for-the-cause-articles/four-steps-to-take-board-members-from-fear-of-fundraising-to-enthusiasm* . Use these tips for campaign committees, too.

17.4 | Fundraising with "Friends of" Organizations

What are "Friends of" organizations? The term refers to a U.S. not-for-profit corporation that has been granted a tax exempt 501(c)(3) status as a public charity – and which has a primary purpose of raising funds in the United States to carry out activities overseas or make grants to an organization located in a foreign country. The term 501(c)(3) refers to a section of the United States Internal Revenue Code.

Why use "Friends of" organizations? They make donating money easier and more attractive for both U.S.-based individuals and U.S. private foundations, for several reasons, including that the donation to a charity may have tax benefits to the donor. "Friends of" organizations (as tax-exempt charities) may have certain tax savings in their operations compared to other organizational forms. For a discussion of their uses and alternatives see: *http://www.trust.org/contentAsset/raw-data/9ac67b50-b2b2-44bd-8342-bb539bfdcb8d/file* .

Opportunities to serve alumni and supporters. A "Friends of" organization can hold networking, social, informational, and public relations events. While these events advance the fundraising aims of the organization, they also build community among alumni and supporters. In this sense, the organization can function like an alumni regional association abroad (see YaleGALE information on that topic, as well as regional associations in general).

The types of programming and volunteering that promote a sense of community among this set of "friends" also create real friendships. Group involvement can help develop a culture of loyalty to the group itself and the foreign university, even when that is not part of the culture of the university itself. In short, *while usually intended for purposes of fundraising "Friends of" organizations can also help raise friends.*

How does one create a "Friends of" organization? Because creating a corporate entity involves legal matters, the short answer is **get an attorney, and possibly an accountant.** Corporation papers have to be filed with a state. A request for tax exempt status has to be filed with the U.S. government. Many states also require a separate registration as a charity in order to ask for money from people who live there. See *http://www.trust.org/contentAsset/raw-data/9ac67b50-b2b2-44bd-8342-bb539bfdcb8d/file* . The organization does not have to have the words "Friends of" in its name – and some now recommend against that: *http://nonprofitbanker.com/fundraising/are-%E2%80%9Camerican-friends-of%E2%80%9D-organizations-a-thing-of-the-past/.*

Legal regulations. "Friends of" organizations are subject to extensive federal and state regulation, so can be expensive or laborious to establish and maintain. The "Friends of" organization, and its board of directors, must be independent of the foreign organization. The Board cannot all be employees of that foreign university so it is an opportunity to use alumni volunteers. The "Friends of" organization cannot just be a conduit of funds from U.S donors to the foreign organization. The "Friends of" organization needs a broader purpose than just channeling funds. It must fund specific projects rather than the foreign organization generally. See *http://www.trust.org/contentAsset/raw-data/9ac67b50-b2b2-44bd-8342-bb539bfdcb8d/file* , *http://www.cof.org/content/how-private-foundation-can-use-friends-*

organizations , http://www.hurwitassociates.com/l_friends_legal.php , or http://charitylawyerblog.com/2010/11/02/what-is-an-american-%E2%80%9Cfriends-of%E2%80%9D-organization/ .

Cultural considerations and potential conflicts. The legal requirement of independence and the need to grant alumni volunteers independence and authority may be difficult for foreign universities not used to a culture of volunteering or independent volunteer associations. The dynamics and challenges of fundraising within the U.S. culture of giving may not be understood by an overseas institution. Understand that money will not just flow in: every charity competes for donations with other charities – and competes for the volunteers' time and talent. The administrative costs (whether in dollars or donations of time and talent) can be substantial to establish and to maintain the organization. In addition, foreign institutions need to be aware of U.S. political and cultural norms and that university actions affect the willingness of U.S. donors to give. In addition, a "Friends of" organization cannot (as a charity) be involved in lobbying the U.S. government, or participating in U.S. politics. Actions of "Friends of" organizations have constraints, including restrictions on grants that might be perceived as falling under "anti-terrorist" guidelines.

To achieve success, the overseas institution must be committed to support, coordinate efforts with, share information with, provide resources to, and thank volunteers for the "Friends of" organization. Giving notice when university professors or officials are visiting the U.S. is invaluable. Providing speakers from the university can be priceless.

Chapter 18

The Role of Volunteers in Fundraising

Volunteers can be a key to fundraising success. They are not just unpaid help. They set the tone and expectations of a fundraising campaign in ways that professionals cannot. However, though unpaid, volunteers are not costless. They require a commitment from the top of the organization. They require significant organizational time, effort and resources in order to be effective.

Volunteer fundraisers help with access and signaling. Alumni volunteers know people you do not. They have access to people you may not. People who do not trust you, may trust them and be persuaded by them. A volunteer's involvement in a fundraising campaign signals something about the value of your organization, and talking about their involvement will have ripple effects in the community: *www.afpnet.org/ResourceCenter/ArticleDetail. cfm?ItemNumber=22464* .

Most fundraising volunteers also donate their own money to the campaign (not just their time and talent). Their donations signal to their peers (as well as the more affluent) what is an appropriate gift – in a more immediate and cognizable way than anything that a professional fundraiser can say. Even though a small percentage of donors generate most of the donations, the level of giving of the rest of the donors – including the visible volunteers – can set expectations for the more substantial givers.

"People give to people, not causes." So says one consultant, when stressing the power of a personal solicitation by a volunteer fundraiser – especially in the context of maximizing leadership gifts, in capital campaigns. Some recommend that a volunteer seek gifts at his or her own level of giving. (Matching asker and prospect is key.) Some suggest that the best solicitation is from a personal friend. For many of the largest gifts, a wealthy volunteer fundraiser can make an effective "ask" of a friend that a professional simply cannot: *http://www. cdsfunds.com/category/volunteers* .

Volunteers are often people who have benefitted from the organization. Their involvement is itself a testimonial. What they say as part of a donation request is likely to be more compelling and emotionally resonant (even if less polished) than a professional's pitch.

Managing volunteer fundraisers. Give volunteers clear expectations. Build a tight interconnected network. Don't overwhelm volunteers, rather give them focused tasks. Train and equip them well. This is as important as training your fundraising professionals. Keep the volunteers' eyes on campaign goals. Keep volunteers above the details that staff can do better – your volunteer fundraisers should focus on securing financial pledges and commitments of time from others. Make them look good. And of course thank them. For a much expanded discussion of these issues, see *www.cdsfunds.com/leading_ leaders_effective_volunteer_management.html* . See also a study on best management practices for retention of volunteers: *www.urban. org/uploadedpdf/411005_volunteermanagement.pdf* by the Urban Institute, as well as *http://www.ssireview.org/articles/entry/the_new_ volunteer_workforce* .

Much like paid staff, volunteers need to be offered milestones, check-ups, and sometimes even pep talks. Time is always of the essence, and unlike money, time is a precious non-renewable resource. A highly-valued volunteer, one who is particularly effective, resourceful, enthusiastic, and galvanizing, especially needs to be managed. Often, they are sought by multiple institutions to be a lead volunteer. If you don't treat and manage them well, they will volunteer their time, talents, and treasure elsewhere. If this volunteer is spread thin, staff needs to be strategic about its requests. Determine who on staff has a talent for working with volunteers.

Commitment from the top. The leaders of your organization must be involved in your fundraising campaign – from the President of the University or Chair of the Board of Directors on down – often in different capacities than alumni relations or development professionals. Otherwise, if the leaders' actions and words demonstrate that they view this as someone else's responsibility it sends several disastrous messages to staff, volunteers, and prospective donors: their efforts aren't that important, they aren't that important, and their donations aren't that important. See *http://www.raise-funds.com/1999/how-to-recruit-your-volunteer-fund-raising-team/*.

Everyone knows the importance of valuing volunteers and thanking them – even if most don't do it. Because almost no one likes to ask others for money, one of the few ways for leadership to acknowledge the value of volunteer fundraisers is to be among those participating in the asking.

Volunteers can be the difference between good and great fundraising campaigns. Certainly paid staff bring discipline, vital structure, and daily effort to raising money. But volunteers, working with strong staff, can bring sparkle and immeasurable momentum to any fundraising effort. Volunteers are the people who get to, want to, and choose to give their time, talent, and, in the best cases, their treasure too.

Chapter 19

The Arc of Giving over a Lifetime

The Pareto Principle in fundraising (that a small portion of the donors give the vast majority of the moneys raised) implies something quite misleading. It suggests that development efforts be focused on the few people who have a lot of money to give. To be blunt, this suggests that fundraising professionals devote almost all of their time and energy to people in their mid or late careers, after they have become wealthy – and that the only young people worth cultivating are the internet billionaires. However, if time is not spent nurturing a habit of giving among your alumni – a culture of giving back – then when they have resources to give, which is often later in life, they will not feel connected to the institution so they will give in smaller amounts or to a different cause.

Teaching alumni to give starts when they are still students, continues when they are young adults with little to give, and persists through the ups and downs of life. It is not just that one doesn't know who will accumulate wealth. It is also that the habits of giving are learned from one's classmates and peers.

19.1 | Preparing Students for a Lifetime of Giving

Students and young alumni feel more connected to each other than to the institutions they attend(ed). Studies are showing that younger donors and volunteers give time, talent and treasure out of a sense of this interconnected community and extended "family" rather than a traditional sense of charitable obligation. This is why it is so important for the university to help build this community – and be perceived as an integral part of it. In contrast, when the university is perceived as apart from, inimical to, or disdainful of this community, its members will feel no obligation or desire to give back to university. Also, young donors are more results-focused in their giving – they want to know with specificity what results they "get" when they give.

Building an interconnected community of students starts when they are accepted at university – if not before. The actions of the admissions department, departments providing services to students, and offices of student life can positively (or negatively) effect the subsequent efforts of development and alumni relations. Give students email addresses for life, create life-long virtual communities, and support student activities that foster community. This goes beyond institutional help setting up or maintaining student activities. It also includes personal involvement of faculty and administration in student lives (see Residential College Masters at Yale, or involvement of Yale Deans and Provosts cheering on university sporting teams). Teach students that the reason they had such a good school experience is because of the generosity of their predecessors. If they are not having a good experience, fix it. If the community of students feels divorced from the university, there is little for which the school can effectively solicit.

Make alumni part of every student's interconnected community. Have successful alumni mentor and teach current students in a variety of settings: on campus and off, in large groups and small, in official courses and casual get-togethers. The on campus, small group, casual get-togethers are particularly important in establishing intergenerational connection and providing models of alumni success that include coming back and giving back. It's important that alumni speak about what they've done since graduation. It is essential to demonstrate that giving back time is as important as giving money – and that one's relationship with alma mater does not end when one graduates.

Have students interact with alumni – as many as possible. Discuss with students what it means to be a good alumnus or alumna. Have students involved in alumni solicitations, thank-yous for donations, or both. Have recipients of named scholarships connect with donors. See *http://giving.yale.edu/news/giving-yale/students-celebrate-giving-elihu-day* .

Those who give large gifts begin by giving early. Certainly, not every early giver will become wealthy enough to donate a fortune, but the importance of reaching current students and young alumni cannot be overstated. Among those who make a gift of over $500,000 to Yale, the vast majority made their first monetary gift within 5 years of graduating. This is why Yale has focused in recent years on educating students about the gifts that make their Yale experience possible, and on executing a broad-based Senior Class Gift campaign.

Involving current students in fundraising – both as donors and as solicitors. If you train dedicated students (alumni-to-be!) to reach out to their classmates for an annual fund gift, you've won half the battle in instilling a culture of giving for a lifetime.

❑ **The Senior Class Gift.** At Yale, students finishing their undergraduate education are asked to pledge their first contribution to Yale during a three-week campaign in February of their senior year. Graduation is typically in May. Consequently, sentimental attachment typically runs high as students begin their final semester. To build the habit of giving, the act of giving something is more important than the amount.

❑ **The Senior Class Fundraisers are fellow students.** The people doing the asking (Class Agents) are other Senior Class students who personally know the people whom they ask for gifts. The askers are volunteers who know the givers because they live in the same Residential College. Effort is made to have Class Agents solicit people they know best. Class Agents are given training in how to ask, especially about emphasizing participation. Following graduation, Class Agents may solicit gifts from their classmates for decades.

Use friendly competition to drive increased participation. Students at some schools (such as business schools) thrive on competition per se. Students elsewhere may respond to competitive "challenges" against rivals.

❑ **Competition among Residential Colleges (dorms).** At Yale both undergraduate social life and non-varsity intramural athletic competitions are based on the Residential Colleges – this fosters a friendly rivalry among them. During the Senior

Class Gift Campaign, the seniors in each Residential College "win" a matching gift if they achieve certain goals or challenges, including reaching participation targets, increasing participation over the previous year, and raising the largest dollar amount. For information on matching gifts see: *http://en.wikipedia.org/wiki/ Matching_gift* .

❑ **Competition "between" classes.** There are also challenges for the entire Senior Class with respect to raising more money or increasing participation over the previous year's graduation seniors. With this friendly competition, participation has risen from 83% in 2004 to 97% in 2014. Total dollars raised has also increased.

❑ **Online competition.** For an online, game-like approach to fundraising see *http://vimeo.com/52150696* from SSE-Riga.

19.2 | Keeping the Connection with young alumni

Ask for what young alumni can actually give. Young alumni may have little to give financially – so set giving levels that are appropriate, yet would still be a stretch. This encourages recent alumni to think about considering the school a priority in their charitable giving. Involve them as a community of both askers and givers – so their friends are doing the asking. Engaging students to participate as fundraising volunteers helps to build a team of alumni fundraising volunteers. Ask for time, talent, enthusiasm, and attendance when there is not yet treasure.

You can't ask them if you can't find them. Do you have valid contact information for your young alumni? Young alumni are far more mobile than older alumni – *hence, the importance of an email address and a cell phone number.* The one address that doesn't change when young people change apartments (or zip codes) is their email address. (Their parents will forward hard copy letters for only so long.) Develop and implement a strategy for obtaining email contact info and cell phone numbers.

- Give alumni (and students) email addresses for life.
- Hold "free" real-world events, where admission requires an email address.
- Raffle off the latest technology item and collect email addresses on entry forms (notify winner via email!)

    Breaking through the spam and clutter. Most email is spam: *http://en.wikipedia.org\wiki\Email_spam*. Much snail-mail is junk (*www.nytimes.com/2012/09/20/business/seeking-revenue-postal-service-plans-to-deliver-more-junk-mail.html?_r=0*). Your solicitation can get lost. The issue is not just getting one email read, but losing a contact.

- *For email - an eye-catching graphic, a snappy subject line, or short text that's brief and to the point.* 47% of all emails are opened on a smart-phone, 19% on a tablet: *http://marketingland.com/34-percent-email-opens-now-happen-pc-83277*. 64% of people say they open an email message because of the subject line (Chadwick Martin Bailey: *www.cmbinfo.com*). Some suggest that the entire email should fit, plain text, on an iPhone screen with no scrolling.
- *Handwritten "thank you" notes still work.* Young people may be tech-savvy, but they appreciate the time that handwriting a note takes.

    Build a virtual community – *if you can't get your message to them, let them come to you.* Try to connect with young alumni where they're spending time. Phones are primary. On average, people check their phones 110 times a day (*www.npr.org/blogs/alltechconsidered/2013/10/09/230867952/new-numbers-back-up-our-obsession-with-phones*). YouTube sees a spike in activity during primetime shows – this is a multitasking generation. Email, LinkedIn and Facebook may be a minimum requirement. Instagram is encouraged (*http://news.yale.edu/2013/12/10/yale-makes-mark-instagram*). E-newsletters can keep your alumnae/i up-to-date on current university affairs: *www.nytimes.com/2014/06/30/business/media/for-email-a-death-greatly-exaggerated.html* (see the bi-weekly e-newsletters of Yale President Salovey in Notes from Woodbridge Hall: *http://president.yale.edu/speeches-writings/notes-woodbridge-hall*). The ask is in the context of community.

❏ *Use social media to create online communities for students that will last a lifetime.* New students are more likely to join than alumni (alumni opt-in 20% to 35%, incoming first years up to 95%). Some forms of social media use institutional email addresses as a form of authentication. This allows the university to create private online community spaces without the bother and expense of providing its own authentication services. However, if student email accounts are deleted upon graduation, these community spaces may disappear – unless graduates opt-in (or sign up) again, and unless alternative authentication is employed. Neither of which is easy or costless. Keeping these communities intact is one of many reasons to provide email for life. Another is that an intact school email address for life outsources some authentication without monetary expense.

❏ *Social media is about relationship building.* Keep your institution relevant by constantly updating your social media presence with new information. Do something with the information you gather from social media. Are people contributing to your School's group discussion on Facebook for whom you don't have valid contact information? Have they given to the School in the past 5 years? If not, reach out. Your goal is to turn 'followers' into 'givers'. Do not rely on social media as the primary vehicle for making your solicitation.

Use social media as a vehicle to inspire real-world action or attendance at real-world events. This includes attending reunions! Design marketing and fundraising campaigns to go viral, but realize that one cannot predict what will go viral. When soliciting online – couple giving with actions (but see *http://vimeo.com/52150696* from SSE-Riga).

❏ *The ALS Ice Bucket Challenge* raised $94.3 million between July 29 and August 27, 2014. (People post videos of being drenched with ice water online to raise awareness.) Compare with $2.7 million raised during the same period the previous year: *www.alsa.org/news/media/press-releases/ice-bucket-challenge-082714.html* .

❏ *The Barack Obama 2012 re-election campaign* had 45 million Facebook fans and raised over a half billion dollars online: *http:// swampland.time.com/2012/11/15/exclusive-obamas-2012- digital-fundraising-outperformed-2008* .

19.3 | Keeping Alumni Engaged over a lifetime

When alumni experience financial success, they may be asked to give more. Often a fundraiser (professional or volunteer) will learn of career, family, or financial achievement during a cultivation conversation. That's one reason that such conversations should be open and wide-ranging. Many donors that have recently achieved financial success will be motivated to increase their giving through these thoughtful discussions.

When life makes alumni question their giving, fundraisers must work to keep them engaged. Like a marriage, a lifetime of giving requires maintaining the relationship in good times and bad. Otherwise, a donor may develop a habit of not giving, or of giving less. Discovering a prospect's concerns or changing circumstances is a reason why personal communication is so important. It can reveal a problem in time to fix it – or ameliorate its impact. An important part of a fundraiser's job (especially a volunteer fundraiser) is strengthening the donor's relationship with a giving community, because this can affect the interconnected feeling among those in the community as well as giving by others.

❏ **Hard times.** Individuals who have come on hard times can be moved by the idea that their participation at any level sends a powerful message especially in support of a community with which they identify.

❏ **Less remunerative work.** Some occupations and professions just earn less than others. For example, this may be the case with people working for government or not-for-profits. All donors and their gifts matter and their contributions are a message that every student is significant, every field of study and professional field is valued, and every gift is important and a vote in support of the school.

❏ **Retirement.** Retirement occasions many changes in lifestyle and spending. Still, it is an opportunity to affirm that the donor is an important member of this community, and will continue to give at a level which is comfortable. It is also an opportunity to discuss testamentary and "life income plan" options available that could benefit both the donor and the school.

❏ **Disappointment with university actions.** These are often felt as a personal rejection of the donor – and the donor's most heart-felt beliefs. Some may feel that a university is too political or not political enough. Some may be concerned that the politics, policies, research, or faculty actions are too liberal or conservative, too far left or too far right. Some alumni will feel that the university is not effectively supporting an athletic team or other student activity that was dear to them. Most personal is when the university does not admit a graduate's child.

The fundraiser should first acknowledge the hurt. Then, possibly offer examples of multiple views from the donors' own classmates. Help donors acknowledge (a) how much they have valued being a part of this extended university family, (b) how this "family" has made them what they are, (c) that whatever the disappointment, in the context of the wide range of university opinions and actions, this is not a personal rejection, and (d) that their gift is still a vote that matters to the health of this "family".

When university success offers an excuse not to give. The donor can be reminded not only that the education, research, and services offered all cost more than the tuition received – but also that in economic downturns or difficult financial times for the university, it cannot rely upon increases in tuition, research grants, or government funding. Instead, it must often look to its own husbanded resources which are likely to suffer during economic downturns as well.

❏ **University wealth.** Some donors may feel that the university is already rich enough – and doesn't need more. Explain how the majority of existing endowment is committed to specific efforts. Explain that new gifts support new efforts, new initiatives, or more scholarships. But remember, that's why universities ask, not why people give.

Skeptical graduates of means who are approached by a close, respected friend can be persuaded to make important gifts. This is especially true when the prospect is reminded of individual reasons for support that include, "For me, access to our school's premier experience depended on financial aid and the generosity of alumni who came before me." A small gift can be quite meaningful.

❑ **Needs of other charitable endeavors.** While the value and importance of helping other worthwhile organizations should be acknowledged, the fundraiser can ask the donor to include the university among their charitable priorities. A fundraiser can also point out how much the university helps to address those same causes, from university research, teaching or outreach programs, to the work of classmates and other members in the alumni community. Examples of fellow graduates making a true difference in public office, leading at not-for-profits and in companies, and serving around the world can serve as a reminder of the importance of outstanding education to enable alumni to address social concerns.

"Many institutions promise to change the world for the better, but for my money, our school delivers more often on that promise." *This quote and others adapted from a Yale Law School Fund Volunteer Guide.*

See also 10.2 Parents as donors and community members

Conclusion

If you are reading this or using it for reference, you probably already agree that alumni relations and fundraising are important to your institution and that an organized, thoughtful approach can bring significant benefits. This book can be your guidepost to some of the pathways of a successful volunteer driven organization, particularly one that has the advantage of an alumni population. Yet this book, like the organizations it discusses and examines, is constantly a work in process. While the basic mission of YaleGALE, the mission of your organization and the concepts introduced in this book may change only slightly, structures and techniques will evolve over time to reflect new thinking and new technology.

The overall theme of this book and the consistent need is for person-to-person discussion and action. This is what volunteer organizations are about – and what YaleGALE was designed to promote.

The Yale Global Alumni Leadership Exchange, as its name implies, was founded on the idea of promoting face-to-face interactions and discussions – about exchange and sharing, about talking amongst individuals. As we at YaleGALE gained experience, we found it helpful to produce the written materials collected here to form this Guide. They comprise a "take away" so that YaleGALE conference participants can better recall the topics discussed and the contents of the discussions themselves. Just as importantly, the task of creating the materials provided an opportunity for Yale alumni to focus their own thoughts on these topics. But now, as a collected body of work, this Guide stands on its own, and enables YaleGALE to share its experience with a wider audience.

As a reminder, there are still more resources on the YaleGALE website. We hope to update, revise, and add to this Guide from time to time. However, the latest materials will be on the Resource section of the website. There are also materials written by others, or for other organizations, which have been posted (with permission) to the

YaleGALE website. Such materials have proven valuable, but are not included in this Guide.

Most of all, not everything that YaleGALE does can be encapsulated in a book.

While this Guide can teach much about working with volunteers, YaleGALE provides much more. YaleGALE interactions convey the enthusiasm and competency of volunteers and their volunteer leaders. You have to experience that in person. So we invite you to attend one of our Forums or Exchanges. We hold one every year in New Haven – at Yale in November. We also hold them elsewhere around the world. For information on upcoming events see the YaleGALE Forums website: *www.yalegale.org/forums* .

To get a sense of past events, read Exchanges, the YaleGALE newsletter: *www.yalegale.org/newsletter* .

For more specialized needs, YaleGALE offers consulting services to educational institutions. For more information on these services write *ygale@yale.edu*.

Finally, feelings of community and their emotional energy are at the heart of sustaining volunteer organizations. They are the matrix that binds alumni and volunteers together and keeps them going. They require personal interactions involving mutual focus on a common task. No book alone can generate them. These personal interactions too have to be experienced – and continually nurtured.

Best of luck in your journeys and exchanges.

Ben Slotznick and Kathy Edersheim

Appendices

Appendix 1

Bulldogs Across America Data comparing local programs

All of the Bulldogs programs have much in common.

❏ All programs have either an alumni mentor assigned to the student intern, or an alumni family.

❏ All programs provide FREE housing for interns.

❏ All programs have students living at a local university, where there will be other students.

❏ All programs have organized group activities that introduce the student interns to each other, to the alumni group members, and to the local community.

Three of the programs partner with alumni from other universities and offer internships to students attending those schools.

❏ Cleveland: Case, Colgate, Ohio Wesleyan, Smith, University of Chicago, and Yale

❏ Denver: Brown, Harvard, Middlebury, MIT, and Stanford and Yale

❏ Minneapolis: Wesleyan and Yale

City	Name	interns	alumni	city pop	metro pop
Louisville	Bulldogs in the Bluegrass	30+	450	750,000	1,500,000
Cleveland	Summer on the Cuyahoga*	50+	851	400,000	2,000,000
Denver	Bulldogs in the Rockies**	30-40	1716	600,000	2,600,000
Minneapolis	Bulldogs on the Lakes	10+	1514	400,000	3,400,000
Houston	Bulldogs by the Bayou	30	1059	2,200,000	6,200,000
New Orleans	Bulldogs in the Big Easy	24	524	370,000	1,200,000
Santa Fe	Bulldogs in Santa Fe	15	716	70,000	150,000
St. Louis	Bulldogs by the Big Muddy	8	766	320,000	2,200,000

* Originally called Bulldogs on the Cuyahoga
** Now called Bulldogs In the Rockies/CLIMB or just C.L.I.M.B.

City and metro population figures from Wikipedia, rounded up
Information from years 2011 to 2013

Appendix 2

Study Guide of discussion topics

YaleGALE forums, exchanges, and conferences are built around group discussion, where all participants are encouraged to ask questions and share their experiences in alumni relations and volunteering. Most often, the discussion sessions are organized on a specific topic addressed by a panel followed by open conversation about a list of questions that all participants (panelists, moderators, audience members, and discussion facilitators) should consider. Below is a partial list of topics that have been discussed. Most have supplemental information written for them. See chapters of this book or *www.yalegale.org/resources/ handouts* , *www.yalegale.org/resources/overview-of-yale-volunteering/*, and The Resource Book (*http://www.looksetveritas.com/yalegale/ resources/wp-content/uploads/2012/08/ResourceBook2012.pdf*). They are grouped by major themes that echo chapters in Parts II, III, and IV of this Guide.

Volunteers (developing them) — *Chapters 6 and 7*

❑ **Volunteer engagement**

Topic: "Cultivating the Alumni Connection" – How do you get young alumni to start participating? How do you get new participation among older alumni? How do you keep the regulars coming back?

❑ **Engaging reunion volunteers by showcasing their talents**

Topic: "Case study: Class of 1970, 40th reunion" – How do you recruit class artists and musicians to help organize a reunion? How does this differ from other volunteer engagement?

- **Engaging reunion volunteers to build attendance**

    Topic: "The Attendance Committee" – How do you promote a reunion or homecoming? How often do you send reminders? What media do you use? What about people who can't afford to come?

- **Leadership cultivation**

    Topic: "Motivating Volunteers to be Effective Leaders" – How do you recruit and motivate alumni to volunteer their time to create and run successful alumni organizations? How do you keep alumni involved for the long term?

- **Ways to recognize and reward leadership**

    Topic: "Using awards and recognition to motivate volunteers, cultivate volunteer leadership, and build a culture of volunteering" – How do you distinguish between awards? How do you choose a time and place to present awards? Who should present awards?

- **Governance: Empowering volunteerism through responsibility**

    (see below for details)

Governance and organizational set-up (creating organizations) Chapter 7.3, see also Chapter 2

- **Strategic planning in alumni relations**

    Topic: "Unique aspects of planning for an alumni relations organization" – Who are your principle stakeholders? How does the mission promote giving of time, talent, or treasure? How do you get alumni engaged in the process and make sure they become advocates for the plan?

- **Advanced Strategic Planning**

    Topic: "Generating Bold Ideas" – How do you mine current activities and external peers for new ideas? How do you solicit big ideas from alumni? How do you screen ideas by organizational mission and capabilities? How do you keep the ideas coming?

- ❏ **Regional conferences and convocations**

    Topic: "Producing a volunteer-run conference" – Why hold a conference? How do you choose a venue? How do you line up speakers? How much help can the university provide? Who puts it all together?

- ❏ **Chapter Structure and Management**

    Topic: How can chapters (regional associations) create strong governance structures? How should the individual chapters be structured? How can chapters be financially self-sustaining? What events work best for chapters? Is there a role for international chapters?

- ❏ **Steps in Creating an Alumni Association**

    Topic: What are the planning steps necessary to create an effective alumni association? What are appropriate governance models? How do you make your alumni association great?

- ❏ **Governance: Empowering volunteerism through responsibility**

    Topic: How do governance rules help volunteers develop the capabilities and capacities that they may not realize they have? Where does an organization's vision come from? Why is it essential? How do you put the right people in the right seats?

- ❏ **Alumni Involvement in Institutional Management**

    Topic: What contributions can alumni make to university planning and activities? How do you train alumni to best be able to contribute?

Building community (inculcating values) – Chapters 10 and 14

- ❏ **Cultivating a Culture of Giving Back**

    Topic: How can we train students, while they are still on campus, to be a lifelong part of the institutional family? How can we as alumni better engage with students?

- ❏ **Family Engagement**

    Topic: Brainstorming session: How can we best engage with student families? What should that relationship look like? What are the examples of parental involvement in the U.S.?

❏ **The influence of architecture on university life**

Topic: Can the design of the campus and its architecture nurture student connections and community? How can they create memories that drive alumni to come back and give back? Can campus architectural choices be used as teaching materials? How can they inspire future architects and developers?

❏ **Bridging the Undergraduate / Graduate School Divide**
(see below for details)

Communications – Chapter 11

❏ **Alumni relations and social media**

Topic: "Effective use of social media in universities for engagement and development" – How has social media changed the way alumni engage with their university? How has it changed the fundraising landscape? Which social media tools have been the most effective? How do you run an internet fundraising campaign? Does the internet eliminate the need for other alumni activities?

❏ **Converting a student tradition to an alumni one – and globalizing it**
(see below for details)

Planning events – Chapter 12, 13 and 14

❏ **Reunions and Homecomings**
(see below for details)

❏ **Engaging Alumni of Differing Ages**
(see below for details)

❏ **Regional associations**
(see below for details)

❏ **Engaging reunion volunteers by showcasing their talents**
(see below for details)

❏ **Regional conferences and convocations**
(see below for details)

Reunions, Homecomings, Events (Classes) – Chapter 12, see also Chapter 3.1

❑ **Reunions and Homecomings**

Topic: "Event Management: Planning Successful Reunions and Events" – What are the steps in creating an event that alumni will want to attend? What are appropriate venues and price points? How do you divide responsibility between professional staff or volunteers?

❑ **Engaging Alumni of Differing Ages**

Topic: Why would young alumni be interested in attending alumni events? Why would mid-career or older alumni be interested in attending? How do these groups differ? What are their needs and expectations? What are the best type of activities for each group and how should they be marketed?

❑ **Engaging reunion volunteers by showcasing their talents**

(see above for details)

❑ **Engaging reunion volunteers to build attendance**

(see above for details)

Regional Associations or Clubs – Chapter 13, see also Chapter 3.2

❑ **Regional associations**

Topic: "Sustaining Regional Associations, both Large and Small" – How do you tailor your programming to the size and reach of your association? What can the large regional associations learn from the small ones? What can the small regional associations learn from each other?

❑ **Regional associations abroad**

Topic: "Far From Home: Organizing Regional Associations Abroad" – What are the particular problems facing regional alumni associations located in countries different than the home of their university? What are the hidden strengths? How do you capitalize on those strengths?

- ❏ **Regional conferences and convocations**
  (see above for details)
- ❏ **Engaging Alumni of Differing Ages**
  (see above for details)

Graduate and Professional Schools – Chapter 14, see also Chapter 3.3

- ❏ **Bridging the Undergraduate / Graduate School Divide**

    Topic: "The Graduate School Dilemma" – How do we engage graduate school students in alumni relations? How do we create a sense of identity amongst graduate school students? How do we communicate to graduate student alumni the value of alumni networks and activities such as reunions?

Shared Interest Groups (Affinity Groups) – Chapters 8 and 15, see also Chapter 3.4

- ❏ **Affinity groups (shared interest groups)**

    Topic: "Organizing Alumni Activities around Shared Interests or Identity" – How do you create alumni networks based on common interests such as athletics, theater, or music or shared vocational interests such as law, journalism, finance, or entertainment? How do you find alumni with common interests and get them together?

    How can you use the concept of service to motivate the organization of an Affinity Group? How can you use an Affinity Group to organize service projects?

- ❏ **Organizing Alumni by their Interests and Passions**

    Topic: How do you organize people based on their passions? How do you organize alumni who want to do now, an activity they did as a student?

- ❏ **Converting a student tradition to an alumni one – and globalizing it**
  Topic: How do you use social media to create a multi-locational global event that will enable alumni to participate in what had been a student tradition. How do you organize a global party? How do you organize a global service project? (Case Study of Feb Club, and aspects of Day of Service)
- ❏ **Organizing alumni based on a passion for travel**
  Topic: How do you create programming for alumni who want to travel? How do you turn student traditions into travel programs? How do you use travel as a motivation to create an alumni community? How do you bring service into the mix? (Case Study of Yale Alumni Chorus, Yale Alumni Service Corps, and YaleGALE, with reference to Yale Educational Travel)
- ❏ **Organizing alumni communities based on love of competitive sports**
  Topic: What are some different ways that athletics nurture an alumni sense of community? How can alumni participate in addition to being spectators? Can alumni compete against each other or against students? (Case Study of the Yale Dernell Every Fencing Tournament)

Service Initiatives – Chapters 3.5, 11.3, 13.3.1, and 16

- ❏ **Exploring Opportunities for Alumni to Engage in Community Service**
  Topic: How can we expand upon the community work already being done by individual chapters? How can community work be incorporated into an overall alumni relations structure? What might be new and innovate programs based on service?
- ❏ **Service in the home country and abroad**
  Topic: "Day of Service around the World" – How do you create an event that instills alumni solidarity while nurturing the "call to service"? How do your alumni abroad use that program as a way to connect with the local communities?

- **Travel programs that promote service**

    Topic: "Globalizing the Call to Service" – How do you initiate a service abroad program? How do you involve alumni in its operation and administration? What are the benefits to the University? How do you bring the "call to service" back home?

Student/Alumni programs – Chapters 3.6 and 13.2

- **Mentoring, student-alumni programming, internships**

    Topic: "Bulldogs: Student Internship Programs that fuel Alumni Participation" – What are the components of a summer student intern program? What is the alumni involvement? How do you get employer buy-in? Why involve not-for-profits and NGOs? How do you involve them? How does this train students to give back?

- **Alumni Helping Students**

    Topic: How can alumni engaged in business help foster and develop internship opportunities? Are there other ways to have alumni counsel and/or assist students in their career development?

- **Alumni Strengthening Industry Ties**

    Topic: How can alumni engaged in business help foster and develop university ties in their industries? How can an alumni association increase involvement of alumni in certain professions?

Fundraising – Chapters 17, 18, and 19

- **The Role of Volunteers in Fundraising**

    Topic: How can we strengthen our development efforts? How do we build the ability of alumni volunteers to assist in fundraising activities?

- **Integrating Alumni Relations and Fundraising**

    Topic: How can an effective alumni relations program lead to successful fundraising? What are the steps in creating a successful annual fund? How do you motivate volunteers to be effective fundraisers?

- **Fundraising among students and young alumni**

    Topic: "Creating the groundwork" – How do you lay a foundation for giving while alumni-to-be are still students? How do you teach students to ask their peers to donate? How do you nurture giving in young alumni when most still have little to give? How do you build the relationship?

- **Maintaining the relationship – a lifetime of giving**

    Topic: "The Arc of Life and the Art of the Ask" – How do you (or a volunteer fundraiser) respond to changes in a donor's financial status? How do you (or a volunteer fundraiser) answer the hard questions that alumni may ask?

- **Volunteers in Capital Campaigns**

    Topic: "Developing a multi-year campaign" – How does a capital campaign differ from annual fundraising? How does the role of a volunteer differ?

- **Fundraising in the U.S. for educational organizations abroad**

    Topic: "'Friends of' organizations" – How do you start one? How does this differ from a "club" or alumni association?

Appendix 3

Editor Biographies

Ben Slotznick '70, '73 Dra

Ben Slotznick is a lawyer, an inventor, a software developer, and a real estate developer. Ben has been on the Board and President of charitable and non-profit organizations in his community, including his synagogue and a non-profit housing development for the elderly. As a volunteer for Yale, he has served as President of the Yale Club of Central Pennsylvania, which covers an area the size of Scotland but is sparsely populated by Yale alumni, and currently serves as Co-Secretary of his Class. Ben is on the Board of YaleGALE and Chair of its Communications Committee, for which he has produced the award winning YaleGALE@Yale (of which he is the founder) and two YaleGALE trips. Ben has organized an award winning Class Reunion and the award winning YaleGALE website. In 2014, Ben received an AYA Leadership Award (Volunteer of the Year).

Ben also attended the Yale Drama School. He later obtained a J.D. from the University of Pennsylvania Law School and Ph.D. in Public Policy Analysis from the Wharton School, where he conducted laboratory and theoretical studies in game theory. Some of Dr. Slotznick's research, which focused on small group interactions, was published in peer reviewed journals.

Kathy Edersheim '87

Kathy Edersheim is Senior Director of International Alumni Relations and Global Programs at the Association of Yale Alumni. At AYA, her specific responsibilities include Yale Educational Travel and the three global mission programs, YaleGALE, YASC (Yale Alumni Service Corps), and YASA (Yale Alumni Schools Ambassadors), as well as being part of the management team. Kathy is also working on a metrics project to assess alumni engagement. She is the founding Chairperson of YaleGALE and produced five YaleGALE trips prior to joining Yale. As a volunteer, Kathy was a Board Member of the Yale Alumni Service Corps and produced their program in China and their first program in Ghana. She was Vice-President of the Yale Alumni Chorus and co-produced the Celebration of Song Tour in 2011. Kathy served on the AYA Board of Governors for four years. Kathy was the first woman President of the Yale Club of New York City – the largest college club in the world with a 22 story building located in the heart of midtown Manhattan – and continues to serve on the Board of the Club. Kathy won the AYA Volunteer of the Year award in 2008. In 2011, Kathy was awarded the Yale Medal, Yale's highest award presented by the AYA, conferred solely to honor outstanding individual service to the University. Prior to joining AYA, she worked as a Financial Advisor and marketing professional. Kathy received an MBA from the Stern School of Business.

Praise for The YaleGALE Guide

"I'm in awe! What a useful document. It is very dense but full of extremely useful insights. Clearly very much about Yale's way but so much is actually universal. I would be very surprised if there wasn't something of use to anyone involved in alumni relations wherever they are based. ... I would certainly wish to share it with colleagues."

— *Michael Mitchell, Secretary of the General Council, The University of Edinburgh*

"When I received the YaleGALE Guide, it was a pleasure to read all the tips and words of advice around programs and volunteer management. ... The Guide gives a picture of all the possibilities in connecting with the alumni of one's institution, keeping in mind that fundraising is an integrated part of alumni relation management. ... The YaleGALE Guide will help me and my colleagues at the University of Amsterdam to further develop our alumni and fundraising programs!"

— *Carolyn Wever, Director of Development and Alumni Relations, The University of Amsterdam*

"As a descriptive, as opposed to a prescriptive, presentation of the range of activities volunteers who want to support a university can pursue, the YaleGALE Guide offers a rich resource of ideas and suggestions, useful across cultures and continents for all kinds of academic institutions. It is an informative smorgasbord in the best sense of that word."

— *Dr. Gregory S. Prince, Jr., Board Member of the European Humanities University and former President of Hampshire College,*

"The YaleGALE Guide is a must-have for universities serious in fostering alumni relations. Yale is widely considered as the Gold Standard for development and engaging with alumni. The Guide lucidly explains Yale's approach and the variety of programs to match alumni interests and needs of the university. The strong emphasis on volunteer leadership for alumni leadership is an important lesson for us. ... The Guide will help universities like us to emulate Yale's mantra of success."

— *Ravi Sinha, Dean (Alumni & Corporate Relations), Indian Institute of Technology Bombay*

Made in the USA
Middletown, DE
11 October 2016